BEYOND LEAN PRODUCTION

BEYOND LEAN PRODUCTION

Emphasizing Speed and Innovation to Beat the Competition

Roger G. Lewandowski

CRC Press
Taylor & Francis Group
Boca Raton   London   New York

CRC Press is an imprint of the
Taylor & Francis Group, an **informa** business

A PRODUCTIVITY PRESS BOOK

CRC Press
Taylor & Francis Group
6000 Broken Sound Parkway NW, Suite 300
Boca Raton, FL 33487-2742

© 2014 by Taylor & Francis Group, LLC
CRC Press is an imprint of Taylor & Francis Group, an Informa business

No claim to original U.S. Government works

Printed on acid-free paper
Version Date: 20131025

International Standard Book Number-13: 978-1-4822-1582-3 (Paperback)

Library of Congress Cataloging-in-Publication Data

Lewandowski, Roger.
    Beyond lean production : emphasizing speed and innovation to beat the competition / author, Roger Lewandowski.
        pages cm
    Includes bibliographical references and index.
    ISBN 978-1-4822-1582-3
    1. Lean manufacturing. 2. Manufacturing processes--Cost control. I. Title.

TS183.L47 2014
658.5'1--dc23   2013032776

Visit the Taylor & Francis Web site at
http://www.taylorandfrancis.com

and the CRC Press Web site at
http://www.crcpress.com

Contents

Introduction

I want this book to be a conversation between you, the reader, and me. I will start by introducing myself. My name is Roger G. Lewandowski. I am a former president for Carrier Air Conditioning operations in Canada. We took the operation from a losing division to a profitable division in only 18 months. I was then promoted to Carrier's largest division, Residential Heating and Cooling, with sales of $2 billion a year. Records were set, many of which have not been broken today.

I have been a leader and a troubleshooter my entire career. I started World Competition Consultants (http://www.wcconsultants.com) after taking an early retirement in 1993. We have 35 proven specialists who I call business doctors. They are more than just consultants. They have at least one degree and a minimum of 10 years of experience. They can address any problem our clients might have, and our business doctors make house calls.

Our specialties are moving or consolidating factories (we have moved over 20 to date) and rapid business turnarounds. We believe that speed is critical, and that timely action, if addressed properly, not only will bring quick returns but also will build a healthier Lean company or corporation.

My mission is to gain your trust to the same extent you trust your family doctor. I want you to succeed even further than you have. My intention is to share with you proven secrets we use for manufacturing success and the tools that we use to build that success. My organization wants to be your coach, assisting you to win this global war.

Lean manufacturing must continue to be implemented in all American factories. Many factories in the United States have a Lean manufacturing person responsible for its implementation. I think this is wrong. The person should be a resident coach and teacher for the corporation. But, the individual responsibility must stay with the managers of each department in the office or the plant. The Lean coordinator must report monthly the progress that each manager is making to the president and what was accomplished. The leaders again must be responsible for continuing improvements, not the coordinator. It is a serious mistake having the coordinator be responsible for the factory.

In my opinion, American industry is only operating at 65% effectiveness in truly implementing Lean manufacturing. Even though progress is being made in the United States, there is still much to be done.

One other point that I want to bring to your attention is that many factories and offices are trying to implement Lean improvements on processes and layouts that are obsolete. This is a serious problem. We must remember that American factories overseas can also train their employees with lessons to be learned in Lean manufacturing.

So, what is your answer to win this battle? The answer is that they cannot compete with you on speed in delivery to the customer. When you deliver to your customers in a matter of hours or less than a week without huge inventories, you can be invincible. So, you must use the following to make changes where feasible to your factories using speed in all that you do to take care of your customers.

The answer to American industry is speed in all that you do in the office and the factory, eliminating all waste and concentrating on making the customer happy with your service and quality as well as cost.

Our competition overseas is fighting the cost of operating overseas, costs involving everything from the containers they ship, loading and unloading, and time lost in getting a product to the customer. This added cost will continue to rise. If we do what I am suggesting in this book, business will be forced to come back to the United States. Competition overseas may have no option but to move factories to the United States. I am going to share with you 13 tools that are critical. You must adapt them to your facility where it makes sense. I will keep reminding you throughout the book that speed is our secret weapon, and the simplification of bureaucracies can be the added value.

We need a holding action that will put together the disciplines needed to run your business and where you are in developing your business. You can choose the options that will best fit your business strategy to stay competitive and to make the eventual change to a business command center.

In Phase 1, I share with you the various tools and tactics that you can use to fit your present situation.

Phase 2 includes an advanced business command center that is new in the industry. You will discover revolutionary ideas that no one has used. It is a breakthrough in manufacturing.

When these two accomplishments are complete, you will become truly world class.

Additional materials for your use are provided in "Further Information and Homework."

The only way the competition can survive is either to purchase your company in the United States or to bring more of their factories to the United States. When you accomplish the holding action and the introduction of the business command center, you will be unbeatable. This will revolutionize American industry by giving your customers powerful products with outstanding quality at the lowest cost possible delivered with the ultimate speed. Yes, you can do this, and I can help you.

Phase 1

Holding Actions

INTRODUCTION

In this section, we discuss the tools that you can use to compete while you prepare to make the changes that will allow you to proceed to Phase 2. We discuss the tools that you can use. However, you must decide the ones that will fit your products and processes. The purpose is to make you even more profitable. If there is a problem with which you need assistance, call me, and we can discuss it at no cost to you.

HIGHLIGHTS OF KEY ITEMS

1. Propose a holding action plan to hold off your competition while you are rethinking your business.
2. Rethink who you are and what type your business really is. Perhaps you will see that this is a time for change or expansion.
3. Rethink your objectives, mission statement, business plan, strategies, and tactics.
4. Decide which actions you are going to take that fit your team on the tools in Phase 1.

Caution: I believe Americans can beat anyone, as we have proven in the past. But, we must face the reality that manufacturing as we know it is becoming obsolete. Automation, robotics, continuous flow, and root cause assessments will be major tools for the future. Henry Ford was the first revolutionist in manufacturing. We have continued to improve his ideas and processes. But, I feel that we are entering a second Industrial Revolution that is going to change the way products are designed, tooled, and implemented. We do not need to work harder. We need to work smarter. We are going to have to retrain our employees as well. Many of them are going to need training for computer applications. We also must make new applications in designs that can be used worldwide to absorb the labor force.

While we are developing new strategic approaches to the basics of business, we must continue to be aggressive in the marketplace and compete with what is available. I call this a *holding action*.

You must focus your attention on the 80/20 rule to buy time with the people and processes that you have in the market today. The principle of the 80/20 rule says that 20% of your customers make up 80% of your volume. You must concentrate on them and ensure that you are giving them excellent service and quality in a timely manner. If you can have superior quality compared to your competition, customers will be willing to pay extra to acquire that.

The Toyota strategy is successful because people assume its quality is better and therefore will pay more for a Toyota. In addition, you will see this in used car lots. People will pay more for Toyotas, which is a powerful marketing perception. The competition is learning from Toyota. It is to be seen if Toyota can maintain its number one position in quality, which again shows you that you cannot rest on your laurels. You have to continue finding ways to make your product exceptional.

There are various tools and strategic weapons that you can use to become more competitive depending on your present situation. Each factory and office has its own culture. You must customize what you are going to do to fit your culture; again, based on your design and products, you will have to select the correct tools. I now review the tools you can choose. In some cases, the tools are applicable for all offices and factories.

HOLDING ACTION FIRST

I am suggesting that you have a Phase 1 holding action against your competition. In addressing Phase 1, I share with you 12 secret tools that you can use in your business. Every business is at a different stage of development and has different needs. So, you and your team can decide which tool is appropriate to use in your stage of development.

These steps are critically important:

1. Propose a holding action plan to hold off your competition while you are rethinking your business.
2. Rethink "who you are" and what type your business really is. Perhaps you will see this is a time for change or expansion.
3. Rethink your objectives, mission statement, business plan, strategies, and tactics.
4. Decide which actions you are going to take using the 13 tools in Phase 1.

TOOL 1: CONTINUOUS FLOW MANUFACTURING

Ninety percent of the layouts used today for manufacturing are obsolete. What we see happening is that most are trying to implement Lean manufacturing on obsolete layouts, many of which are 10–20 years old.

Continuous flow manufacturing is necessary. It is part of the answer to beat world competition. I mention this several times throughout the book. Speed is a competitive weapon. It is our answer to beating the competition because we can give the customer what the customer wants in 24 hours or less. Our competition overseas cannot do that.

Figure 1.1 shows the normal flow in the average American factory. Figure 1.2 shows a new layout using continuous flow manufacturing.

One of the keys of continuous flow manufacturing is the use of single-minute exchange of dies (SMED) to reduce setup times to less than 10 minutes. Also, there will not be the major stockrooms that you have today. The material will flow to the point of use. Kanbans will be used where needed for safety stocks. However, this is on the line, not in a storeroom.

Purchased parts will be delivered to the point of use and stored on the line. They will have a maximum of 2 weeks' supply on purchased parts.

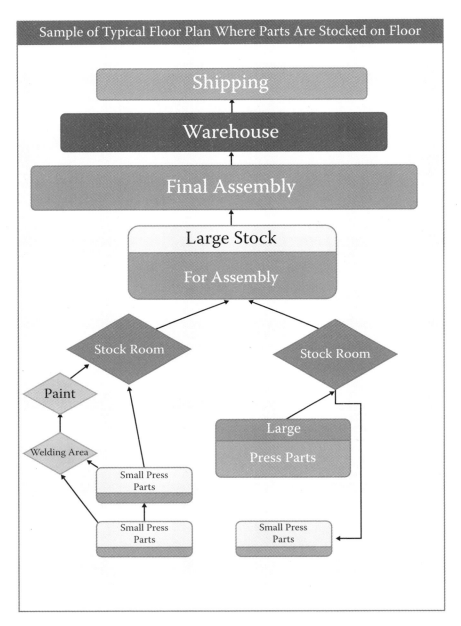

FIGURE 1.1
Sample of typical floor plan where parts are stocked on the floor.

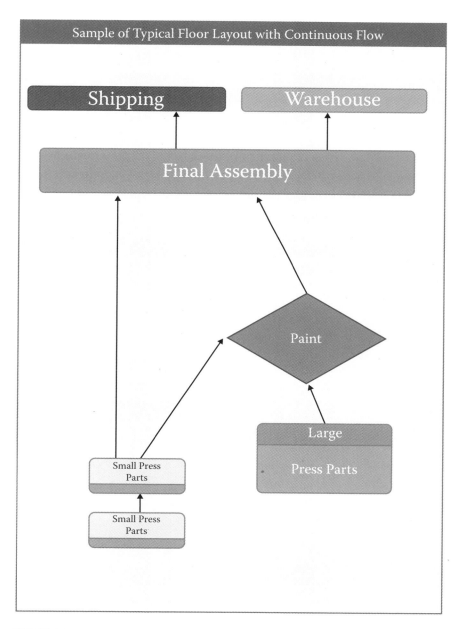

FIGURE 1.2
Sample of typical floor layout with continuous flow.

TOOL 2: HIGH-VELOCITY WORKING CAPITAL

High-velocity working capital becomes successful through a team strategy to minimize all inventories and to reduce company payables. The objectives are to *use speed as a competitive weapon* and to *eliminate wherever possible any obstacle that interferes with increasing inventory turns.*

High-velocity working capital is not just inventory; it is the total working capital in dollars as a percentage of revenue dollars. This gives you the working capital per dollars of revenue as a base point to establish a new target.

To establish a base under this umbrella of high-velocity working capital, the following provides starting points:

    I. Working capital consists of inventories of the following:
      A. Raw material
      B. Work in process
      C. Finished goods
      D. The company's receivables less its payables
   II. Reducing working capital yields two powerful benefits:
      A. Every dollar freed from inventories or payables frees up a one-time dollar contribution to cash flow.
      B. The quest for zero working capital permanently raises earnings. Like all capital, working capital costs money; reducing it yields savings. In addition, cutting working capital forces companies to produce and deliver faster than the competition, enabling them to win new business and charge premium prices for filling rush orders. As inventories evaporate, warehouses disappear. Companies will no longer need the amount of forklift drivers or indirect people to handle inventory or schedulers to plan production months in advance.
  III. *The most important discipline of zero working capital is speed.* Many companies today still produce large amounts of scheduled parts in the factory. This ties up the factory, not cycling the parts that are needed in a timely manner, causing overtime and excess inventories and the risk of obsolescence. This is a great opportunity for corrections if you are scheduling large quantities of parts through your equipment.

IV. Minimizing working capital allows organizations to demolish the old system, scrapping forecasting and building to order using strategic kanbans internally and with suppliers.

This is the introduction to our objective. How do we begin this process? In the following section, we consider action plans.

I. The first and most critical action is to analyze each part. Each will have a unique strategy that will determine its strategic use. Ghost numbers (partially finished parts that can have multiple uses) need to be considered. Ghost numbers allow manufacturers to react quickly as needed for certain assembly.

II. On items that do not require a lengthy process, point-of-use manufacturing needs to be set up as much as possible.

III. On key parts, strategic kanbans need to be set up so that items can be replaced in a matter of hours or days. These kanbans will allow a shipment in 24 hours on standard items and a matter of only weeks on special items. It can be done.

IV. On the items that are not the "bread-and-butter" items, there is no need to stock finished goods. However, the materials that cause the lead times to be several weeks or months need to be analyzed to see if a kanban can help slash the lead time.

V. Continuous flow is imperative. This means that manufacturers must rethink plant layouts. Products must flow to minimize the need of inventory storage. This will also create savings because there will be fewer fork trucks and less indirect labor.

A. Receiving materials are identified and marked by color and location number so that they can be delivered to the point of use promptly without confusion. This eliminates lost time spent hunting for the parts and reduces storage and handling.

B. A supermarket is used when there are a large number of SKUs (stock-keeping units) produced with widely varying demands and rather short acceptable lead times. For the large number of SKUs with low volume, it is important to hold a small kanban of their raw materials and to be able to access it quickly when needed. All other parts go directly to the assembly area.

C. The general stockroom will only handle parts that are used in several areas of the factory.

D. An analysis of the cost of producing parts internally versus their price for purchasing outright (mainly on standard items in the industry) is imperative to check which cost is best.

E. All processes, including machining, welding, painting, and the like, must be evaluated strategically. All key processes should be addressed first by process utilization, which many times is surprisingly ignored by management as part of the norm.

Our unique Process Utilization Form is simple, but powerful. This can be computerized for ease of analysis (see Figure 1.3).

F. Rethink the distribution warehousing of inventory items and, where possible, ship directly to a job site or distributor warehouse or ideally from the assembly line to the customer direct, eliminating the items going to the warehouse and saving money.

G. Any finished inventory over 45 days old should be discounted or scrapped.

H. The total paperwork system needs to be simplified by using process planning. This will simplify paperwork required to do business with the customers. In process planning, duplication is eliminated, and speed and accuracy become critical factors. All paperwork flow should be computerized for improvements and reduction to simplify the complexity and time needed in processing customer sales orders. You can do this by using process mapping. In process mapping, you chart each step in the process as it is being done today to identify lost time and steps that can be removed. The end result is all manual reports and actions are changed for simplicity and standardization.

In summary, these actions are going to require training of individuals to implement them. The good news is, as all of the employees are being retrained, the employees will become more valuable and motivated to be involved in this revolution with new ideas.

During this retraining process, every employee needs to focus on quality for every item, process, and assembly, including those in the office. Whatever the number of employees (200, 500, 1,000, etc.), all will individually be responsible for the quality of his or her step in the strategic operation to supply customers with what they want when they want it. Quality is checked, verified, and tested on all items. This will

Process Utilization

356 S. Calderwood St.
Alcoa, TN 37701
Ph one: (865) 681-0029
Cell: (865) 414-9009
E-Mail: Roger@wconsultants.com
Web site: www.wconsultants.com

Date:
Machine:
Building:

"Specialists in Rapid Implementation"
Royal Ventures Corp.
Roger Lewendowski, CEO

Record all Down Time

Working Hours	Part Number	Order Qty	Qty Made	Time Start	Time End	Time Down	Reason
1							
2							
3							
4							
5							
6							
7							
8							
9							
10							

FIGURE 1.3
Process Utilization Chart.

reduce warranty cost and repair cost greatly. If needed, there should be a root cause analysis for design or tooling to simplify and eliminate this cost.

The goal is to have the best and the longest warranty of anyone in the marketplace. When customers think of quality and durability, there is only one name that qualifies: yours.

High-velocity working capital is a total team effort of all employees, shipping, and distribution. Everyone should take pride in doing his or her part. Management is replaced if they fail to achieve quality in their job description. You must "walk the talk."

High-velocity working capital, accompanied with superb quality, is the ultimate defense weapon in the marketplace regardless of global competition.

Conversation and brainstorming are needed to identify the steps required to obtain the quickest results to the bottom line.

The key focus is to rethink the processes of controlling inventories, raw materials, work-in-process inventory, and finished goods. They must all be in a constant state of flow to the customers.

TOOL 3: PROCESS UTILIZATION:
TOTAL TEAM GAME PLAN

The total team approach is powerful, deceptively simple, and very affective. On the plant floor, for every process, there is a simple Process Utilization Form on a clipboard. The hourly person clocks in on the clipboard and records what the job is and how many pieces he or she has to run. If there is a shutdown for any reason, the person must list the time shut down and the reason. This becomes powerful real-time information. There is no need to wait for computers. This can be used for all key process, such as painting, welding, machining, as well as the assembly lines.

The plant manager, supervisors, and the supporting people for maintenance, materials, or quality cannot go home until they meet and decide what corrective actions must be taken tomorrow for improvements. This not only is recorded in real time but also action on these items will be taken by the designated accountable people the following day.

There are many benefits:

Everyone knows the objectives. Also, many times you find out that there is a need for additional training. For example, in the past we have found that a certain maintenance person can fix a machine in an hour, while another might take 3 hours. We saw the same thing in machining and welding areas on setup. It becomes exciting because rather than punishing an employee, the employee is given extra training, making the person more efficient and proud.

It is fun as well as effective. Make work fun for the employees with special prizes. In the past, we have given pizza parties for areas that excel as a whole team, and we have given individual awards and entries into monthly drawings. These drawings could be for fishing rods, golf clubs, tennis racquets, dinner for two, and other things.

In one factory, the names of the winners of the monthly awards were reentered into a large box. After 6 months, there was a drawing for a used pickup truck. The truck was put on display for the entire factory. The winner drove the truck away. It was very effective and exciting. It was recognition for work well done. We made a tremendous improvement in teamwork and quality while reducing cost. We changed the culture to be very positive, saved a tremendous amount of money, and left those in the facility with a "can-do" attitude that continued the process.

TOOL 4: PULL SYSTEMS

Push Your Production Forecast out the Door and Pull in Customer Satisfaction

Traditionally, production scheduling relies on the old standard practice of taking the sales forecast, applying capacity available, and placing it into some sort of sequence. These forecasts are generally a combination of customer orders and input from salespeople or, in some cases, customers regarding what they think may happen. Often, the business relies on historical data. Material is pushed through the process, and, more often than not, these forecasts are just plain wrong. So, how do we avoid the push? Implementation of a pull system is the answer to this dilemma.

A pull system, implemented properly, can truly allow you to pull customer orders through the system without adding inventory based on forecasts. Using kanbans for type A models that you know will move can balance the production more effectively than building to a forecast. The operating philosophy becomes that you build what is needed to fulfill either the orders or the kanbans and then you stop. You do not push inventory. You allow orders and kanbans to pull requirements through your operation.

Pull systems used in this fashion have several inherent benefits. First, excess inventory is eliminated. The mindset of "if we build it, they will come" can be dangerous to your cash flow if it leads to high inventory levels. Second, the possibility of obsolescence is greatly reduced because you have less inventory on hand. Third, quality problems and their impact are lessened because if there is a problem, your exposure to scrap or rework is greatly reduced as the on-hand quantities are much lower. Fourth, you can expect that space reductions will be made because there is less material in process or in finished goods. Finally, with the order pull through and the kanbans, you will likely see your lead times reduced (an 80% reduction

Summary of Pull System

Action	Benefits
1. Reduce lead times by a minimum of 60%	Powerful marketing and sales tool.
2. Reduce floor space by 50%	In-house room for new products or warehousing.
3. Reduction of in-process inventory by 50%	Less handling and storage needed.
4. Increase inventory turns by 100%	Increasing velocity in manufacturing saves cash flow and borrowing of money.
5. Implement WCCs unique Kanban system (secret)	Eliminates the need for MRP in scheduling; use MRP only for business planning.
6. Eliminate surprise shortages	Average factories today lose 10% of their capacity. Labor costs increase by 5% when waiting for needed materials.
7. Simplify software needs and systems	Eliminate 50% of computer software and electronic scheduling using visual factory techniques. The employees will be able to control scheduling and production needs.
8. Have at least 25% less handling and storage of inventory	Freeze hourly head count replacements. Let attrition reduce the workforce or use the extra people for a new product you can acquire. This provides huge savings and better costs.

is not unrealistic), while your on-time customer delivery performance increases as well (we have seen instances when this rose to 98%).

World Competition Consultants (WCC) has had great success with this approach and would like to suggest that you use our unique strategy on kanbans as you implement this process. When a kanban signal fires, we do not recommend that the kanban be automatically filled. The replenishment signal needs to be reviewed by a materials professional planner to determine if it needs to be refilled based on the long-range material requirements planning (MRP) plan or product life plan or whether there is a seasonality to the product that may be occurring. Kanban systems without this review tend to respond too late to both rising and falling trends in both directions. In addition, we suggest you consider establishing kanbans on hard-to-acquire or problematic components.

TOOL 5: ROOT CAUSE ANALYSIS

Root cause analysis is probably one of the most misunderstood tools and is often not used in manufacturing. In most cases, management recognizes that it is a serious problem if quality defects are passed on to the customer. Highly capable engineers specialize in getting quality out to the field. They design elaborate test stands and put in special equipment to test the product going out. Rejects are put into repair lines. Schedules are missed because of poor quality, and overtime is required to try to pick up on what needs to be done. This is more typical than the exception.

We have just completed working with a Fortune 500 company on a quality issue. Our "business doctor" went into the quality area, and instead of trying to improve on the quality testing, he went through three factories and used root cause analysis as his tool. Where they had weld failures, he eliminated them all. He also eliminated all paint delamination. Where they had wiring problems, he eliminated all possibilities for miswiring. He went back to find the root cause of each problem and corrected the design parts so that they could not be misused. He helped redesign the parts that were being welded to eliminate the potential for failures. This one individual working in three facilities saved over $1.5 million annually using root cause analysis. Perhaps oversimplifying what he did, he helped redesign the item so that it could only be used one way and went through the process so that it would be capable of repeating the process to simplify its capability of repeating quality items.

The point I am making is that if you can get to the root cause of quality problems, you can redesign the parts, simplify the process, and save a tremendous amount of money not only in house but also for the problems in the field. In this case, we did not even attempt to calculate how much we would save in warranty cost, which would be tremendous as well.

Root cause analysis should be used throughout the factory and offices where there are bottlenecks, such as order entry being too complicated. Root cause analysis should be a way of life for the entire operation, with monthly meetings to determine where a root cause analysis must be used to save time and money simplifying the process.

TOOL 6: SINGLE-MINUTE EXCHANGE OF DIES

Single-Minute Exchange of Dies (SMED): "Reduce Your Setup and Adjustment Times from Hours to Minutes"

SMED is so critical that it cannot be discussed in just a page. I would recommend that you purchase the book *A Revolution in Manufacturing: The SMED System* by Shigeo Shingo (New York: Productivity Press, 1985).

The heart of the JIT (just-in-time) method is quick changeover methods. Shingo, the inventor of SMED for Toyota, shows how to reduce your changeovers by an average of 98%. By applying Shingo's techniques, you will see rapid improvements (lead time reduced from weeks to days, lower inventory and warehousing costs) in quality, productivity, and profits. The book is a marvelous source of ideas and contains hundreds of illustrations and photographs as well as 12 in-depth case studies.

According to Shingo, a simple approach to achieving a quick setup and changeover of the dies can be achieved by the following:

Maximizing external activities
Converting internal activities to external where possible
Engineering or streamlining all remaining internal activities

Massive gains have been achieved using the SMED system, as illustrated in 1982 at Toyota, when the die punch setup time in the cold-forging process was reduced over a 3-month period from 1 hour and 40 minutes to 3 minutes.

SMED is important to your success. I hope that I have motivated you to examine Shingo's book. It is a revolutionary tool that must be studied in detail from the original source.

These modern times of rapidly increasing diversity, smaller batch sizes, and setup time reduction are crucial for the profitability of many companies. For example, bottling industries sometimes spend more than 20% of planned production time on changeovers. Fortunately, these setup and changeover times can be reduced significantly when the SMED system is applied. As an example, if you preheat the oven before cooking a pizza, the actual time the pizza is in the oven is dramatically reduced.

Continuous Flow Manufacturing

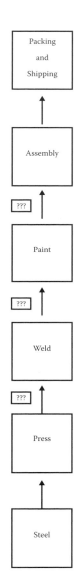

A. Using SMED will reduce setup times to less than 10 minutes. This will speed up the process times.

B. Using mini storage sat next point of use will reduce about 80% of present storage space required.

C. This layout will drastically reduce the need for handling personnel.

D. This will create a huge inventory savings in dollars.

FIGURE 1.4
Continuous Flow Manufacturing Chart.

The method's strength is the systematic approach for analyzing what is actually done and how time is spent during the changeover activity. Through the analysis, a better understanding is gained of how to do certain activities when the line is running. Also, what can be done to reduce the fine-tuning activities after the actual changeover is determined.

Changeover losses are one of the six big losses that have been defined within the TPM (Total Productive Maintenance) method.

Special Note: I once had a client who had an extremely large press that took 6 to 8 hours to change the setup. The cost of the press was several million dollars, so a second press was not affordable. I came up with the idea of creating a team of people who worked on the small presses. With a total of four to five people, we reduced the setup time from 6 to 8 hours to 2 to 3 hours. Eventually, with root cause analysis, this time was reduced even further by eliminating small things that caused delays.

TOOL 7: STRATEGIC BUSINESS UNITS

An Old Idea Updated Makes Sense: Saves People, Space, and Overhead

Strategic business units are a tool that takes two factories and puts them into one building, each with its own independent process but sharing only one management team. Setting up strategic business units allows combining manufacturing facilities into one while maintaining the integrity of separate profit centers.

The profit centers can have separate space by putting a temporary screen between the two in the assembly, storage, and other areas. If the backup area equipment is capable of supplying both of the profit centers, it could be set up as an internal supplier, charging each profit center for the internal orders that are produced for them. If the backup area is not compatible, the area can be portioned off as well.

There would be an overall manager for both profit centers in manufacturing and a support staff for both profit centers. The profit centers will use these staff members as internal consultants when and where needed. They will be charged a fee for these services.

If a service is not totally used, then it will be eliminated and will be replaced with outside consultants as needed.

The separate profit centers will have their own sales, marketing, and engineering functions.

Important Points

Before the two factories become one, we must go into each and use Lean manufacturing concepts to reduce the space requirements, improve all processes using process mapping, simplify setups using SMED, introduce strategic kanbans, reduce excess people, dramatically reduce inventory in process, and install velocity manufacturing to reduce internal lead times to hours, not days, and reduce supplier lead times to a matter of days. The results for both facilities would be to enable reduction of lead times on the major products (using the 20/80 rule) to be shipped in 7 days or less. All other items would be studied for component lead times and would ship in a matter of 2 to 3 weeks.

As velocity manufacturing is implemented, using all of the tools of Lean manufacturing and process mapping, you would have a build-to-order system, eliminating the use of forecasting except for overall planning needs.

The key point is that each factory must eliminate all waste and shrink all lead times internally and externally before the consolidation. *It can be done.*

Key advantages that will be accomplished are:

- Inventories will be reduced by 50% or more overall.
- Space will be reduced by 60%.
- Lead times will be reduced for sales by 75%.
- Employees needed will be reduced by at least 30%. The receiving factory can tell its people they will be temporarily laid off. As the new products come in, they will have more job security.
- Overall cost should be reduced by a third.
- One whole set of top management is eliminated by going to one facility.
- They are true profit centers, with all support management internally used as needed only and no large allocations.

The result will be a highly competitive and flexible profit center with allocations.

Conclusion

This is all doable using the fundamentals that are being used today under the total umbrella of velocity manufacturing.

FIGURE 1.5
Total umbrella of velocity manufacturing.

TOOL 8: ZERO-BASED PROCESS MAPPING

Zero-based process mapping analysis is a professional alternative to arbitrarily reducing salary head counts. Instead, you must go through a process analysis that in the end will determine if there are extra head counts and where they are in the process. Therefore, in the final analysis you will not have voids and confusion.

In this process, you will end up with an organization that is leaner and more nimble and will be energized to move more quickly, with more enthusiasm. Last, it will eliminate marginal employees.

The approach used is simplified into measured steps:

I. First, review with the senior management person to see if there is a possibility of combining positions and eliminating positions and identify any marginal people in top management. The reason that we need to start at the top is, once management has agreed to these people being acceptable, any changes that might be recommended will now have a strong foundation for beginning the review of the organization. *They will be our key advisors.*

II. Our next step is to begin the process mapping analysis.

A. This will involve the entire salary group below the top staff (who the top management person has already evaluated).

B. We start with a given discipline that is reporting to one of the staff's senior managers. We would use this person's organizational chart as our guideline for his or her staffing. As stated, this person will be a key advisor, and we will report to this person on his or her areas.

One example might be accounting. We will track and map the entire salary process step by step from the first step in the process. Again, we will be mapping every salary head count reporting to this senior staff person. We will do the same process for every other senior manager's staff based on their organizational charts.

C. We will map the process in detail according to the individual person:
  1. We would reach an agreement with the person on what his or her function is.
  2. We would determine if that function was really needed by asking, Why? five times, as the Japanese suggest, to make sure we reach the core answer after examining the alternatives.
  3. Should the function be changed?
  4. Could the function be combined with another function?
  5. Requirements and procedures change, and there is normally always an imbalance between functions time-wise (not everyone has an 8-hour workload). Many times, the variants are down to a 50% workload. By balancing the workload, we can reduce waste and eliminate salary head counts once we reach an agreement with the key advisor (management staff person).
  6. A new job description is written based on the analysis of each function.

III. Dual mapping must be kept for analysis and presentation. In other words, there should be mapping before and after summarizing the reduction of excess people and reduction of a timeline again from before and after each staff area summarized in head counts and timeline reductions.

IV. As we are able to eliminate or combine operations for the purpose of this analysis, you will mentally put these people aside in a holding position.

V. All managers must evaluate their employees' performance in a descending order of performance. The best employees are at the top, with the marginal at the bottom.

The steps taken in Items I through IV identify people who are now in excess. They would go into a theoretical holding pool of manpower. The managers will then, as a team, take the excess salary pool and across the organization agree on the best place to use these individuals in eliminating marginal employees. The results will be an increase in the caliber of the total team and the elimination of waste (salary head count) that can be laid off. This will make a significant impact in cost saving, increase the caliber of the total team, and reduce timelines.

VI. You must now address the span of control of middle management. By eliminating the excess salary people, certain supervisors or managers now have only two or three people reporting to them. Management must now determine if functions or responsibilities can be combined and certain managers eliminated.

VII. You would again use the approach we did with salary and rank all middle managers in descending order of performance. Then, evaluate the excess managers available against the descending list and replace marginal staff with better-qualified people. These managers who are no longer needed will join the salary people who are also no longer needed for removal.

VIII. Once this is completed, the senior staff should get together as a team to see if they can now eliminate levels of management and become a flatter organization. Here, again, the managers are evaluated, and the least qualified are expendable or, if needed, replaced by a new hire who is more qualified.

The end result is that you now have a new, exciting, motivated Lean team that will have ideas and challenges and achieve greatness beyond your expectations.

Ten Steps to Process Mapping

1. Map the present steps of the process from right to left, identifying the inputs and the outputs of the process.
2. Evaluate the process identifying the weaknesses of the current process.
3. Propose changes to improve the process.
4. Map the process again with the proposed changes from right to left, generating a draft procedure.
5. Evaluate the changes:
   How many steps were there originally as compared to the steps in the proposed revised process?
   How much time was saved in the proposed process?
   How much money (estimated) was saved in the proposed process?

6. Review the proposed draft procedure with the implementation team.
7. Develop a final implementation plan with corrected process.
8. Evaluate the changes:
    How many steps were there originally as compared to the steps in the proposed revised process?
    How much time was saved in the proposed process?
    How much money (estimated) was saved in the proposed process?
9. Implement the new process with training where needed.
10. Continually audit the new process, keeping records of estimated time and money saved.

TOOL 9: STRATEGIC KANBANS

Kanbans are normally thought of as a modern way to control inventories. They replace the old-fashioned use of reorder points and max/min systems in controlling inventories. The truth is, kanbans are misunderstood and misused many times.

I believe that the proper use of kanbans goes much further than controlling inventories. They should be used as temporary bandages for a process that needs to be rethought or redesigned.

It is difficult in today's world to accurately forecast building products for the marketplace. I would say in most forecasts you are lucky on an annual basis if you are 75% correct—unless you peg the marketplace to build the quantity you wish. The danger is that you limit your growth and your capital utilization. The key point is that *forecasting for production should only be a guideline for planning capacities* but not a build schedule.

If you accept the fact that forecasting is unreliable in today's world and could seriously impair your cash flow, you can use finished goods kanbans strategically for your build and sales functions. Use the 20/80 rule and evaluate what your most profitable and best sellers are. These are the items you should ship within 24 hours for a competitive advantage. You set up kanban quantities that build in the replacement time for the kanbans plus an original safety factor that will be fine-tuned as you use this tool. You now can see what your maximum inventory dollars will be as you begin to build on these kanbans.

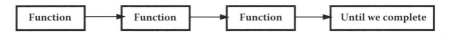

FIGURE 1.6
Continuous flow.

One of the exciting advantages of using these kanbans as a strategic tool, the way WCC uses it, is that every time a kanban is reaching a replenishment point, we demand that the marketplace be evaluated quickly to see which way the trend line is going (up or down) for requiring your product so you are operating in real time. Too many times today, when business is increasing, your inventory is too low, and when business is decreasing, inventories are too high. You are always behind the curve.

The marketplace is a volatile environment. It is affected by seasonality, dumping by competitors, quality problems that affect sales, pricing disadvantages, and more. The exciting part is that if you use kanbans correctly, you are constantly adjusting the kanban quantity on finished goods to your best reading of the marketplace. If you do it correctly, this makes you highly competitive without large cash flow problems.

We have just discussed the use of strategic kanbans on finished goods using the 20/80 rule, which states that 20% of the volume is 80% of your profitability. We now can discuss the 80% of the finished goods items that equal 20% of your business. You cannot carry kanbans on everything, nor should you—a classic error by some management. We still want to give our customers the best lead time on these items without having them on kanbans.

We must evaluate what the items are that make up those assemblies that cause longer lead times, because you want to be very flexible and competitive against your competition, on the purchased items that are used in their assembly. The secret is to get the suppliers to carry the kanbans and deliver in 24 hours. We may have to assist and train the suppliers regarding why and how to set up kanbans, maintain them, and again, check every time a kanban is reordered so the latest information regarding its needs is available.

As a customer, you must establish a discipline for the supplier to report to you that the supplier is, in fact, maintaining your kanbans.

One of the options with suppliers you also must consider strategically is they might have a long lead time from their supplier on a special part or special raw material. If so, as professionals, you may consent to authorize a portion of the kanban inventory cost. Again, if you visualize that we are talking about the 20% that creates 80% of the business, the volume should be low until you have done something to shift it to a high-volume classification (20% equals 80% of the business).

This is simplistically said, and it is not complex to use kanbans as a centerpiece of your strategic planning to be very flexible and highly competitive and control cash flow. Its potential is exciting. You can outthink your competition.

We now should address the manufacturing parts. Again, we should not use kanbans as just inventory control tools. We must evaluate all of the manufacturing parts individually and develop a specific strategy for them. Let me provide a few of the options to consider.

Wherever it is possible, the equipment to fabricate, weld, or even paint should be moved to the point of use so you stamp it out, weld it, paint it, and put it on the product. Again, it depends on the process needed to finish the part, but technology, for example, has given us the option of powder-coating minibooths for painting. Whatever the process in this design for manufacturing, try to use it at the point of use. When I was in Japan, I was surprised to see idle machining equipment in assembly. The Japanese tour guide smiled and said, "We buy used equipment, recondition it, and put it in assembly for point of use, and they would rather have a used piece of equipment sitting idle, that may be for limited parts, than to have the inventory."

On large, bulky items, we should arrange the process so that the second shift makes only enough parts needed to get through the day shift. I call this the "bakery theory." The bakery brings people in early to make donuts, and then they stop for the day. There must be arrangements to handle large parts differently and minimize the stock.

I recall with one client, we had parts that were 4 × 6 feet, and we ended up putting in a press brake. We would have what I call the "blanks" in assembly, and they would form them as required. Whatever the situation is, there is a way of *simplifying it and having it flow to the point of use.*

On the 20% of the manufactured parts that go into the 80% of the volume, if the parts cannot be manufactured at point of use, then they are eligible to be put on kanbans. In doing so, the main criterion for kanban quantities is the built-in time for replacement with a small safety factor. It is critical that every time a kanban is to be replenished, it is signed off by a supervisor in the materials area that the MRP trend, or other tracking software, is used to see if the need for the part is decreasing (due to seasonality) or should be increasing.

The biggest fault with kanbans is that, if they are not properly used and limited, you could lose control of your inventory cost. That is why each individual item is strategically reviewed regarding how that part is made. Is it a point-of-use item, a kanban item, or a build-to-order item?

Kanbans to me are a bandage and should be used only until the correction is made to eliminate the kanbans. Wherever possible, you want the material to flow and not build inventory. Kanbans are a tool to be considered, used carefully where needed, and reviewed quarterly to see what can be done to eliminate them.

From a management standpoint, every kanban must be authorized regarding why it is needed so control of this tool is not lost.

One other option, as you are reviewing the strategic use of each part internally, is to check to see if it makes more sense to purchase that part than it does to manufacture it. We tend not to do this or not to audit ourselves as often as we should.

In today's world of using speed as a competitive weapon and to overcome the fog of forecasting the future, kanbans are especially qualified to limit your risk and, at the same time, accelerate the response to customer requirements.

Also, one of the benefits of using kanbans strategically (internally in manufacturing) is that you can avoid the chaos of tearing down setups for rush jobs or a customer's special request. In many facilities, kanbans eliminate the mass confusion with regard to scheduling needs (the chaos of lost time, overtime, and so forth).

This is considered the duck theory, in that, as you watch a duck glide across the water, it looks so smooth and easy—but beneath the water, the duck's feet are paddling like mad to go forward. In manufacturing, the flow of materials should be like music, and the feet paddling is the strategic thinking done to design for manufacturing, eliminate obstacles, and maintain quality in all that you do.

TOOL 10: ACCELERATED RETURN ON KAIZEN (ARK)

We have noticed that many of our clients have spent a great deal of money and employees' time training these employees in training room situations on what kaizen events are to familiarize them with this tool. In fact, most all books on kaizens relate training as being the first step. It is an accepted practice.

We have studied this with several of our clients after the training has taken place and found the following negative results:

> The retention percentage, after the trainees leave the room and we ask questions regarding what they heard, was less than 50%, and as time passes and they are not part of a kaizen team, the retention factor falls even further. We found this to be true with corporations that had local colleges put on classes for several weeks. But, in fairness to the colleges, we experienced the same results for our 3- to 4-hour training.
>
> As people quit or retire, you need to retrain replacements; this is not normally done in a structured way.
>
> As seniority affects the movement of people within a company, this information (training), again, is lost.

Necessity Is the Mother of Invention

We had a recent experience with a corporation that had three factories, and the corporation was in serious financial trouble. We suggested, based on our experience, that we do something different from the normal kaizen with the training.

We suggested that we have a plant-wide meeting, saying that we would come in and implement Lean manufacturing techniques to reduce cost quickly to stay competitive and survive. We encouraged the employees' cooperation.

Our seasoned business doctor made a quick, walk-through analysis and determined what processes needed to be addressed for the quickest and greatest return. He then made a simple process mapping change, and received input from those in supervision, and showed the employees proposed changes and asked for their input. They immediately took action to make the change and removed all waste (Toyota seven wastes of manufacturing).

As a result of the changes made, fewer employees were required and were employed based on seniority; the extra employees were removed immediately. The extra employees went into a labor pool and were used for special projects or replacements due to attrition.

This gave us a better idea of what the costs really were for sales. There was seasonality in the product line, and at that time, we reduced the labor pool based on seniority; in the future, they will continue to use that practice.

We did not properly record what was to be accomplished, in my viewpoint. We now require this:

a. A simple case study form is used for each task to identify what is to be changed and why.
b. The time started and the time completed are charted on this form.
c. Also, the cost to accomplish this task is recorded.
d. The forecasted savings are recorded (return on investment, ROI).

Summary

I think that the use of ARK (accelerated return on kaizen) is the most realistic and practical approach for kaizen events. Thousands of dollars are not lost on training. The results are tracked weekly to prove that the savings are there. I can tell you that this particular client, not because of this alone, is beginning to see daylight because the client's prices are now more competitive and sales are up.

Using the ARK approach as a tool is critical for a company in trouble and needing urgent action. In a well-organized facility such as Toyota, kaizens are a way of life. The supervisors and management are expected to have continued improvements using kaizens. As I mentioned, the individual in charge of Lean manufacturing should be the coach and should be in charge of documenting weekly improvements to management so that management can judge who the superior managers are. Individuals who are not performing as well can be trained by the Lean coach. If they still are not progressing, they should be demoted or released. The secret at Toyota is the expectation of improvements as a constant way of life. That is the way it should be.

My example that necessity is the mother of invention is only to be used when corporations and companies need actions immediately. Then, once it is done, they should copy the Toyota system of continuous, relentless improvements.

Case Study: ARK

Client: _____

Location: _____

OBJECTIVES

_____
_____
_____
_____

RESULTS

_____
_____
_____
_____

Time/Date Started _____ Time/Date Completed _____

Estimated Cost _____ Estimated Savings _____ ROI Savings _____

Remarks _____
_____
_____

Name _____

TOOL 11: SUPPLY CHAIN MANAGEMENT

In a classic definition, supply chain management is generally described as the entire process, beginning to end, of planning, implementing, and controlling the elements of the supply chain to maximize efficiency, inventory management, and velocity. These elements encompass all movement of raw materials, work-in-process inventory, and finished goods from the point of origin to the point of consumption or sale. The idea for total supply management is that no single link in the chain can optimize inventory management and velocity. It takes every link in total collaboration and orchestration to achieve maximum efficiency and return on invested capital.

Thus, supply chain management must include the planning and management of sourcing, procurement, manufacturing, distribution, and logistics. It takes as a given that the coordination and close communication by all of the vested parties is evident throughout the chain. Generally, supply chain management is comprised of three main elements: strategic, tactical, and operational.

Strategic elements consist primarily of the strategic location and number of manufacturing or distribution centers and the strategic partnership with suppliers or distributors and, in some cases, end customers as well. Other strategic decisions include the information technology underpinning the supply chain management process and decisions on make versus buy.

Tactical elements involve the actual decision making within the supply chain. These elements can be sourcing decisions and contract formations; inventory decisions on amount, type, and location; and transportation decisions regarding frequency and carriers.

Operational elements relate to the actual execution of the planning. These include the daily production scheduling, demand planning and forecasting, sourcing planning and execution, and inbound and outbound execution.

As supply chain management has grown in acceptance as a preferred business strategy, the expansion of third-party logistic companies that specialize in inventory management and distribution into the mainstream supply management is a notable force. Companies have come to realize that these providers offer a toolbox of skills that enable them to do these transactions and movements more efficiently and often for substantially less cost than the manufacturer itself may be able to do.

Third-party logistics management has been a growing component of the supply chain for a number of years, and expertise and guidance they can offer are often valuable. There are many notable companies in this field that are extremely efficient and have seen extraordinary growth. UPS, the shipping giant, has one such operation with myriad optional services. Another logistics giant, Ryder, also offers comparable services and expertise.

Another element in supply chain management and fulfillment is contract manufacturers for products and companies whose core competencies lie in the design and development of products and technologies. Companies such as Microsoft, with its high-power gaming system Xbox, and a host of telecom companies rely on these contract players. One such company, Flextronics, has positioned itself in the mainstream of this niche and has grown into a multibillion-dollar enterprise.

Many companies have developed specific software applications to assist in supply chain management. These include broad-based enterprise resource planning such as that of SAP or Oracle and many more specific specialized self-contained products. Communication offerings often include electronic data interchange packages and many Web-based tools as well.

Successful supply chain management means that communication up and down the chain must have velocity and clarity, and these products are invaluable for making this happen.

TOOL 12: INVENTORY TURNS CONTROL

Every one of the 11 tools already discussed come under the umbrella of quality, simplicity, and speed. Another powerful tool to introduce is inventory turns control, which is critical to success and profitability. Controlling inventory can be like rolling the dice. All kinds of situations can affect inventory turns, which can make profitable cash flow. You should consider having an inventory turns objective on the entire inventory in the process in manufacturing. Make department heads accountable for inventory control dollar targets. This means all purchased parts in house are the responsibility of the materials manager regarding inventory turns.

All finished goods inventory turns belong to the sales department. Now, all management is being measured the same way for cost, inventory turns, speed, and customer satisfaction.

I address the separate opportunities for A, B, and C items.

A Items

When I took over the materials department, we had a serious problem with raw materials. We either had way too much, or we would run out. Our problem was that many of the steel gauges were so similar in thickness that they could be mistakenly used to make an unauthorized part. Another problem was that the scrap factors that the industrial engineering department gave the factory were not accurate, and scrap tickets were not always used. This was a big problem. My solution was to have a good solid materials person take over the control of raw material. It was a full-time job because the person had to inventory various gauges of copper, steel, and aluminum regarding what we really had. We also set up safety stocks (kanbans) with our suppliers. Our materials person would call the suppliers and tell them when to ship the raw materials. If the materials person did not call them, they were not allowed to ship. We were able to reduce stock outs and control the inventory up to 60 inventory turns. For those in the materials area, I had accounting recheck the IE (industrial engineering) standards for all off fall so that we would not have inventory losses.

Because of my ideas, I was promoted to plant manager and then moved on to higher management. But, I suspect these conditions still exist in manufacturing.

B Items

For purchasing, B items were items that were expensive, like motors, compressors, and some electrical parts, such as electrical controllers. We went through each individual item, and the buyer was not to have more than a 1-week supply of these parts. Monthly, we would review the inventories. If there were violations and there was more than a 1-week supply of these items, then the buyers were confronted and told to get in control. The good news is that you could walk the factory daily to check visually to see if there were excess inventory items. If you thought there was a problem, you could go back and talk to the buyer to correct the inventory controls. In some cases, suppliers were shipping ahead of time to help their cash flow.

C Items

C Items are low-cost items such as washers, screws, and the like. Usually, I would try to keep a 3-week supply, depending on the price breaks with the suppliers.

There were suppliers who were spending a tremendous amount of our time making us worry about on-time deliveries.

We identified these supplier problems. We had purchasing tell the suppliers that if they did not correct the problems within 6 weeks, we would have to find an alternative supplier. Most of them complied.

In our monthly meeting, we would identify in reports where the inventory dollars were. We would find where the dollars were not being controlled and would follow up with the buyers until it was corrected. We usually had inventory turns in the 60s. With today's capabilities and tools, a normal profitable target would be 70 turns.

At the end of the month, if we missed our production schedule, we would see where the dollars were and their effect on inventory turns.

This is important. For example, if there is a manufacturing problem and product was not produced as scheduled, this hurt the materials manager's turns. We would quantify that by dollars as a penalty.

On the other hand, if manufacturing could not produce the schedule because of purchased parts, we would calculate that, and the materials manager would be responsible. It is a very motivational poker game.

I came up with an idea to take pressure off for missing the schedule. By scheduling 1 day of the next month's production in the present month from a management standpoint, it provided more cash flow, and everyone was happy. It takes a total team to really maintain inventory control and customer satisfaction on deliveries. I have had many challenging positions. However, in the trenches between manufacturing and materials, it is a tough ball game. There are so many variables that can affect your success.

Each of the disciplines of materials, manufacturing, and sales is critical to the team for any successful operation.

TOOL 13: MALL THEORY

The future is now. I call this the mall theory of manufacturing. Let your imagination go with me:

1. We must rethink our assembly lines. Wherever possible for fabrication or welding, they should be put on the assembly line so that material flows directly from machine to assembly. The paint line should be tied in as well.
2. The objective is to have continuous flow manufacturing wherever possible.
3. Large sheet metal parts will be manufactured so that there is a cushion of 2 or 3 hours only of what is needed in assembly. These backup areas will be the in-house suppliers to their customers, which are the assembly lines. It may even make sense to have outside suppliers fabricate the parts needed in assembly. This is the exciting part of continuous flow. Key suppliers would have small screened-in storage areas adjacent to the assembly lines. The suppliers would deliver parts directly to the assembly line as needed, depending on the part

size and schedule; it will be coordinated with the assembly line regarding what they need and when.

4. These suppliers would be paid weekly based on what was used in assembly and shipped. So, they would have instant cash flow as an advantage of working with the assembly line. They would rent the space they use in the plant for storage of the material.

Other advantages are:

1. These suppliers will be part of the total team and attend production meetings and contribute their ideas to the total team for better services.
2. These key suppliers will have the opportunity to contribute ideas for better designs, tooling, and processing.
3. The suppliers now save a lot of freight back and forth, are paid weekly, and become active in the total facility to maintain quality and customer satisfaction. Inventory turns will probably be in the 70s and 80s. This is a win-win for a corporation with suppliers and the customers with fast delivery and extremely high quality. This will result in the ability to compete with overseas suppliers for customer satisfaction.

SUMMARY FOR PHASE 1: HOLDING ACTIONS

At the introduction to Phase 1, my purpose was that your business must survive and prosper even though some revolutionary concepts are used in Phase 2. These holding actions are not meant to be stagnating. They are meant to have you rethink your business objectively, strategically, and tactically.

All of you are at various stages of enhancing your profits. Your products differ, and your cultures differ. However, you all have the same objective: to increase your profitability to compete against domestic and overseas competitors. I have listed 13 tools for your consideration to be used by your team. You and your team have to choose your priorities and set your pace. You cannot try to do too much too fast.

As a reader of the book, you will have free access to call me at any time and discuss questions or opportunities that you might have. There will be no cost for this.

I believe that this book is original, and that my company is going to give you the wisdom of over 15 years of helping clients become more profitable.

I kept this last point for the end of Phase 1. I believe that it is the most important item that you need to address. The most misunderstood discipline in business today is the purpose of human resources (HR). It varies depending on the working cultures. Historically, the HR department was the clerical area where employees were set up for work and insurance policies were set up. The job of HR was to help management address problems with employees when needed and to process the hiring and termination of people. These individuals have not been budgeted properly for them to contribute. They were looked at as a necessary evil. In today's HR departments, we see an additional action in that everyone is concerned with lawsuits because they seem to be on the rise. The HR department has become more involved with management individually to work with staffs to avoid costly lawsuits. Management many times will give in rather become involved with lawyers.

There is a danger that the HR department can interfere with the functions of management taking care of the good people and building a case for those who really are a problem. In some cases, the HR department overreacts and can interfere. I think it is critical that we pay the people in HR well because they are an important part of the whole organization. They are the glue that holds the organization together. They can be positive and motivational for all of the employees as the honest brokers treating everyone fairly and real contributors to those in management in making their job more successful.

Any action that you take using the 13 tools must review with the HR department, the place where everyone should go for counseling. You must make the HR department the place where everyone can come for counsel, for business, and for personal problems. Those in the department will direct individuals to outside services for problems if needed.

I think that, in the overall management, the HR department is forgotten. Individuals in HR can provide a tremendous service for everyone. They can be good listeners and cannot gossip about what they are told.

Top management must spend time with the HR people to get the feel of the morale and problems that exist. I am convinced that in these times more authority and time must be given to the HR people, not only to avoid lawsuits but also to be the glue that holds the total organization together.

The HR department must work with management to avoid the risk of being sued. But, these individuals should not scare management unnecessarily so that management does not manage their team as it should be managed to be successful.

Last, the HR department should report to the total team on the status of the organization and be able to answer questions that the staff might have for assistance or discipline.

Phase 2

The Business Command Center

INTRODUCTION TO THE BUSINESS COMMAND CENTER

Bold Breakthrough that Will Make You Rethink Your Leadership

There are exciting and revolutionary changes in the concept of management that will allow you to outthink all competition. "Circulatory management" is a powerful reconstruction effort to flatten your organization and restructure your team. Another "new" management concept that will make your team powerful and successful is the "wingman" theory. The business command center will be the umbrella that will bring a significant breakthrough in management. You will have a powerful and highly flexible team. However, management will bring everyone together with monitoring of the marketplace 24 hours a day and 7 days a week.

I include here some unique operational changes that I want you to consider in your analysis. I want to bring management into a direct position and allow them to have more time to focus and manage their operation. I also want to have critical people present in the command center so they are more accountable and available for quick action. Safety, quality, and distribution are only a few examples of work for the new people. This will focus their efforts and give the directors more time to focus on their primary objectives.

A key position unique to the command center is the director of competitive intelligence gathering. Too often in our day-to-day life, we tend to operate on an internal mode without considering the competition, how the competition may react, and how we should act in return to their changes. This addition will lead to all kinds of opportunities.

A new concept of managing the business command center detail will include three computer screens for control purposes. Each screen will show unique information to review at the command center meetings (i.e. budget control status, sales and marketing status, financial profitability status). Rather than tying up top management with presentations, I suggest a screen manager to be responsible for each screen for collecting all the information needed for the daily meeting.

These screen managers will be responsible for collecting and presenting the agreed-on details for each screen. Timing is critical and communication is essential. Therefore, 30 minutes before the command center meeting begins, the three screen managers will meet with the president and chief executive officer (CEO) and will point out the critical items that need to be discussed and reviewed. This will be similar to how the president of the United States is updated every morning regarding what is critical. These short presentations should be in writing so that the president and CEO can make notes for themselves of what they want to discuss based on this intelligence. This will save a large amount of management's time. One important point is, depending on the size of your business, you may not need three screens, only two.

My overall objective is not to entertain you but to challenge you to think about the kind of leader you are. Are you a follower or a bold and passionate leader who wishes to make significant changes? Changes are needed to be a survivor during a brutal part of world history. Americans are known for imagination. We will be tested as individuals, corporations, and as a country. Do not be defensive about what you have but instead be bold regarding what you can be. We must remember that world competition is becoming more educated and will attack us where possible.

A key support factor for business is that competition is growing more educated. We must ensure that our country is educating our most ambitious and intelligent students, or we will be in real trouble. I personally feel that the government, with the help of the schools, needs to sort out the leadership that is needed for the future and send these individuals to a West Point of business, wherever that may be. These people have to be trained and coached by the government. It is my opinion that the government should pay for the education for these people with these skills in return for so many years of service to the country.

We need someone in charge of this. In this case, I am not only saying manufacturing and engineering, marketing, and sales could be included but also foreign languages for the diplomatic field. In our case, it is not the quantity of people in school—it is the quality.

These are only my ideas and are not necessarily correct. The only thing that I am sure of is what we have done in the past is not going to be acceptable for the future in world competition. You leaders have to decide what to do for our future, perhaps with better suggestions than mine.

We must make a giant leap from Henry Ford's days into a space-age technically advanced world.

The concern I have is that we do not proceed with business as usual. These men and women will be all-Americans in education. We must make these academic successes just as exciting as sports stars.

We also must address the fact that we have technology that will be a huge factor for our workforce as we get into the use of robotics and automation in business.

We have a large unemployed workforce. As we gain technology, we have a problem that our hourly workforce has become obsolete. Many do not have computer skills needed in industry. We are going to have to train them on this capability. The world is going to continue to escalate with opportunities in technology. The government is going to have to support this education process. It is better to keep people educated and contributing than having them jobless and supported by the government. Business leaders need to step up with ideas to correct this situation. We cannot allow our country to degenerate into socialism by default.

I am taking advantage of you as an audience of leaders. You have to be a leader to be reading this book. I am trying to motivate you to rise up and become excited about new opportunities. We cannot leave anyone behind. We as Americans have always been aggressive. The whole team has to be involved.

THE BUSINESS COMMAND CENTER

The world is rapidly changing into a competitive capitalist world where all countries want to be industrialized to make any product to sell in the world market. In the past, we have been protected by two large oceans, keeping possible danger from our shores. Today, with the invention of new technologies and new transportation options, we are no longer safe from competition.

Also, the increasing appetite of all humans wishing to increase their standard of living has resulted in the development of an undeclared but competitive war to make products before other countries until hourly wages are as low as 10 or 15 cents an hour.

All people are trainable, and even though there have been some quality problems, they are rapidly correcting them. They are learning to do things with our technology that they purchased and that took us a century to learn and develop. They are turning around and picking up the capability to compete with us in only 3 to 5 years. We will see this war escalate, and it is going to be a very personal war for everyone involved, the same as a physical war is. We will not hear the crashing of bombs and people being killed, but there are certainly casualties taking place. Today, we are already feeling the effects of this world competition, and many executives have become casualties, as have thousands of factory workers. Their jobs have been eliminated or moved overseas. These people are the "walking wounded," who are having a radical shift in their living standard. This is only the beginning of world competition. I have preached for years that all business is war, and only the believers will survive. This is becoming true even faster than I suspected, and we as Americans are going to have to change our designs and processes from traditional methods to beat the competition and compete with their lower costs. More intelligent and simpler designs using less labor must have outstanding quality and service ability. We must have a quicker response to all customers' needs, and the foundation we must build must be outstanding in everything we do and in every step of our process from foolproof design to tooling and manufacturing. This must also include the office workforce and their response to customers' needs with systems and processes. It must be possible for them to provide customers products faster than their competition with better quality than the competition.

China's emerging population, which has made great strides already, is in excess of 1.3 million people. India is the other giant, with a population in excess of 1.1 million. These two giants, India and China, are eating natural resources of iron, steel, copper, and aluminum at a shocking rate. This is compounded by the world's need for oil and coal. In the near future, there is also going to be a shortage of food and clean water as the population grows because of better health care; the next world war may be fought for basic resources such as food and water.

The governments of China and India face a dangerous dilemma. The more people who receive material gains, the more people who are jealous there will be. In addition, which is extremely important to recognize, this worldwide appetite for material luxuries and the invention of TV globally is going to put countries that cannot compete into a precarious situation. Politically, it can end in international revolutions or war because of jealousy and greed.

Therefore, China and India join other countries in feverishly going around the world to buy all the raw material and oil they can, or the corporations that produce it, because they fully realize the risk of their political instability if their people become dissatisfied. This will compound world competition in all businesses. There are going to be numerous unhappy losers in the competition.

My purpose is to set the stage of the present and coming world revolutions in business and in all of its supporting needs. All the manufacturing processes and raw materials must be changed radically because of what I have just mentioned. The scarcity of raw materials is serious. In addition, major processes and organizations are going to make dramatic changes to reduce product cost. Everyone will have to adapt to a new way of doing business to be able to compete and survive in this new world situation.

Currently, American manufacturing is generally stagnated, and while the computer has launched a revolution, its speed and capability are exceeding our capability to really analyze all the data generated today. The workforce is suffering from overload. Targets are being missed because there has been little attention given to competitors now competing around the world for the same limited market.

While we address survival, we must also recognize that what we need is a "holding action" against competitors. They are at our business gates until we can develop a "new approach" to manage our business to beat the competition in the marketplace. This means we must do two things at the same time: While focusing on surviving today, we must also take time to rethink what is needed for our objectives and strategic plans to keep the winning edge and how it will be achieved.

What Is a Business Command Center?

I discussed developing a holding action to buy you time in the real world to develop your business process, objectives needed in tomorrow's world to be successful, and strategies and tactics that should be considered to achieve the objectives. Once you have accomplished the background, fundamentals, and the foundation of your reinvented corporation, then you are ready to take this total reorganization and put it into what I call the ultrastrategic weapon for business. I have named it the business command center. First, let me state where we are before I go into the details of what a command center is and how will it operate.

Our present organizational structures are being used by practically 100% of corporations and companies. The organizational structure has the board chair and the CEO at the top of the chart. Beneath them, in descending order, are the various divisions and their hierarchy used today.

I have tried to research the origin of the organizational chart. The best I could find is that it may have started with the Roman Empire. The Roman Empire grew so large with its legions of armies, there was a problem of changing it from a mob into a highly trained, specialized fighting machine. Its command structure was written and used to function as an organizational force in the world at that time. In industry, we have continued using the descending-order charts and graphs showing organizational structures and responsibilities in the same way the Romans did. The only part we have improved on is the ability to create new organizations faster with modern technology. This obsolete organization needs rethinking so it is less cumbersome and less bureaucratic and provides a flatter organization, regardless of size, that is not only powerful but also highly flexible to the real-time needs in today's marketplace.

Over the years, many innovations in the armed forces have been adapted from military to commercial areas in processes and technologies. In past military days, runners were depended on to communicate between various commands regarding what was happening and what commands should do. Eventually they progressed to cavalry troops. The military kept improving communications; in more modern times, the more staff functions were brought closer to the firing lines of combat to help collect reconnaissance and intelligence to send to command tents in World War I. In World War II, some of the more advanced commanders were in the German army; they had large vans with telephone lines and radios for communication and could follow the German panzer tanks speeding through enemy lines. The Allied commanders took over hotels and key buildings as command centers and tried to have all of the communications come there to discover what was rapidly changing in the battlefield. The Allies were able to gather intelligence rapidly. In the chaos of war, many of the crucial hard decisions were made at the front by commanders who were bold and aggressive. This holds true in business and war.

In business, we also must know the enemy. The top three competitors need to be determined in the business command center. This is discussed further in this phase, but there should be an individual assigned to know everything about the top three competitors who should receive feedback from the field salespeople and dealers with updates on their activities. Are they aggressive? Do they have new marketing programs? Are they having problems in the field with quality and the like?

Include any other important information in real time that can be fed back by the salespeople or dealers via e-mail or direct contact. This individual should be recognized in the corporation as your expert on the top three competitors. The person should use the assistance of everyone and put together a confidential report that states the strengths and weaknesses of the competition versus the strengths and weaknesses of your management team regarding products, service, quality, price, and the like.

These competitive information specialists should always be the sounding board for what the competition might do to counter the action you intend to take. In further discussion about the command center and responsibilities, additional material deals with this person.

Strategically, this input of competitive strengths and objectives should be used in relation to the tactics you want to use to make your strategies work.

This completes your holding action need. You are now ready to move into the Business Command Center.

Implementing the Business Command Center

We now have the foundations and tools ready to insert into the business command center. We must use them in their proper place the same way we would put a puzzle together. They must fit the total picture in the overall organizational culture.

My road map changes the total organization design into a more effective team.

Let us first pause and review what we have today. Generally, we have been using the Roman Army organizational structure of controlling legions from a mob into a precise delegation of culture, with the various layers reporting through channels to the very top. This basic management structure has continued over thousands of years. As our information society has exploded with the use of computer software, we are overwhelmed with information internally and externally in corporations. Management's answer has been to create an even larger bureaucracy with new levels and new titles to handle the information explosion. Another result of bureaucracy in management has added a corresponding explosion of meetings. These meetings resulted in middle management spending at least 50% of their time in meetings with another 25% of their time spent preparing for the meetings, leaving them only 25% of time to communicate with management and their people. This leaves little time for innovation.

The result is not only ineffective management but also delayed communication time needed to answer key customer questions. Valuable counsel is also last for the key customers.

Working long hours and leaving less time for family is the only Band-Aid for middle management. In many cases, these individuals begin to develop health problems and dysfunctional marriages. In many marriages, the spouse feels as though he or she cannot compete with work.

Success is a demanding lover. The more time you give, the more time is demanded. We have reached a critical point in the use of time. We all know the right meetings are critical in any business. I believe the total structure must be replaced using the business command center as the overall umbrella. It cannot operate effectively using the old traditional organizational structure. So, we need to implement a new organization that I call *circulatory management*. All disciplines will report equally to a business command center. This will flatten the organizations and focus emergency attention on their responsibilities in the command center. I illustrate this in a new organizational chart for circulatory management (Figure 2.1). This concept will result in a total team concept. Each management component has its own title. I do not want to designate what titles are used, so here I call all individuals in management a director except for the CEO and chief financial officer (CFO).

Key Points of the Circulatory Management Chart

1. I have added some positions to the command center traditionally subordinate to the director's position. Examples for your organization would probably be quality, safety, and warehousing. It relieves some responsibilities from the director's position and allows the director to focus on his or her key responsibilities.
2. By having these positions report to the command center, they are more exposed and can directly contribute to command center needs. Their tasks will also be quickly accomplished.

FIGURE 2.1
Organizational chart.

3. *Most of competitive intelligence* comes from a new position. This information is to be shared with all of the supporting areas of the organization. All of the support areas must begin to think about what their competition is doing and if they can do better. They may also steal ideas from the competition.

To direct this position, he or she must be a part of the command center. However, they will report to the marketing director to receive directions and will not have a wingman as everyone else has.

Special Points

The financial department represents the CEO, whose wingman is the CFO at the center of the command center. Those in competitive intelligence will report directly to marketing in a subordinate role. These individuals will not have a wingman but are important to the overall command center because competitive intelligence is listed as one of the activities.

Circulatory Management

Circulatory management is a method to flatten the organization. The object of this new concept is to build a team that is highly focused and will respond quickly to any opportunity or problem.

Everyone will be responsible to execute his or her function, but no one will have a personal agenda. Too often in business, a personal agenda will get in the way of teamwork.

The key leaders will bring the command center together. They will be exposed to peer pressure and "visibility." Needed facts must be available so they can contribute to team results.

I do not think the old-fashioned organization can support the control center concept because leaders are no longer kings of their own world. They are now team players.

I am not naive enough to think that circulatory management will stop internal politics.

At the same time, I am also introducing another new concept to the organizational chart. You will notice a connection bar on the organizational chart that says "W-man" between two regularly competitive positions.

To further push the team concept, the connecting wingmen are from an idea from World War II. In the early days of that war, the United States saw tremendous casualties when pilots were in combat. They operated as the pilots did in World War I because they acted as individual pilots. They fought to survive and become aces.

The U.S. Air Force developed a better way of fighting enemy planes. Pilots were divided into two-man teams, so in combat one pilot could attack the enemy while the other watched that pilot's back. The new concept became known as having a "wingman." This concept was extremely powerful and successful. It is still being used.

Adopting this policy will give every director a wingman to be successful. Every director will have agreed-on objectives from the leaders of the command center. The CEO and CFO will be the team commanders.

The team will be judged professionally by 70% of their objectives, and 30% of their judgments will be from helping their wingmen accomplish objectives. Now, they have a meaningful and financial reason to work as a team. All bonuses, stock options, and other fringe benefits will depend on accomplishing objectives agreed on with the CEO and CFO.

There will no longer be internal competition between individuals. However, as the pilots did in World War II, they will become best friends. Their success will depend on the success of others. I believe the secret to making the command center a powerful concept is to destroy old concepts so there will be no other choice but to make the new concept successful.

When the Roman army was conquering the world, they tried to invade England. However, there was a lot of grumbling and fear within the army because the English had a new weapon called a crossbow. This revolutionary weapon could kill from a distance, which made swords less effective. The Roman generals told the captains of their ships to "burn the ships" after the troops were on shore. That meant their only option left was to successfully conquer England. Consequently, they were successful in doing so.

The key to making this total concept successful extends from leaders having the passion to improvise where necessary to make their tasks work. They must beat their competition to survive: Burn the ships and move on to victory.

Business Command Center: Leadership

The command center will be managed by the CEO and CFO as a team. They will make all final decisions based on inputs presented to them. The CEO and CFO will be like conductors of an orchestra. They will not play the instruments but instead will direct everyone to be on the same musical score (action plan).

There may be occasions when one of the commanders will be required to be elsewhere. In their absence, the remaining part of the team will be empowered to make all needed decisions in all major discussions. This may occur if one of the directors is not available for the daily meeting; then, the designated leader will make the decisions. No one is indispensable in the new organization. The CEO or CFO must make the final decision. These individuals can be contacted on conference telephones as needed. Therefore, it is critical for a telephone number to be available to reach all the teams.

The command center meetings should not last longer than a maximum of 2 hours after agreement has been reached on the major items. There may be special reports and update presentations made that will not require all the disciplines there. Once the critical updates and key decisions are made, the directors can request a meeting using the command action for their own department. As you implement the command center, you can adapt it to your culture and business.

1. Financial (CFO): The financial report should include:
   A. The overall financial year-to-date profit versus forecasted profits should be given on line charts showing the last year's actual profits for the same period and the sales year to date. The current year information should also be on the chart.
   B. The charts should reveal the total budget forecast for expenses versus actual expenses.
   C. There should be a review of the departments that are over budget. It should show the budgeted versus actual amount of profits. The directors of the departments must explain their reasons for being over budget and the corrections made.
   D. Make sure a chart includes a summary of the overall year-to-date expenses as a percentage of sales. On the line chart, what is the ratio of the expenses to sales?
   E. Any other financial charts that the team deems appropriate can be reviewed plus any key points the financial director wants to make or questions that need to be included.
2. Quality: Suggested key items are as follows:
   A. The shipping quality as a result of audits of ready to ship items for customers' needs is a necessity in the chart.
   B. Include the actual warranty dollars versus budget.
   C. Display the warranty dollar costs as a percentage of sales. On the line chart, include last year's warranty dollars as a percentage of sales.
   D. What are the defect sales internally on the key process? List the major reasons for them.
   E. Any key information the quality director wants to pass on or question should be included.

3. Human resources:
   A. What is the general morale of the hourly workforce and the salary workforce?
   B. What are the key concerns of the human resources (HR) director?
   C. What is being done to address further education of the workforce?
   D. Are there any concerns about OSHA (Occupational Safety and Health Administration) or environmental issues to be addressed?
   E. Are there key relationships with the community that should be reviewed?
4. Warehouse director:
   A. Is there a backlog in the warehouse of shipments to be made?
   B. How much cycle time is needed from the time of receivables at the warehouse until the product is shipped?
   C. What is the dollar value of inventory? Is there a certain amount that is obsolete? If so, how much is it worth? What are the SKUs (stock-keeping units) involved?
   D. Who are the carriers, and what is their cost today versus the past 2 years?
   E. How much space is being used for warehousing? If there is more than one space, list the locations and the space available. Are they rented or owned? What is the cost per square foot for each warehouse?
   F. Are there any other problems or opportunities that should be discussed?
5. Director of distribution:
   A. Review the list of distribution locations. Be careful to include their address and size.
   B. Are these privately owned distributions? If so, who are they, and where are they located? What selling dollars do they produce? Who are their customers? Are they dealers or a direct, one-step distribution center?
   C. Are there any other problems or information that the director of distribution wishes to communicate?
6. Director of manufacturing:
   A. What is the status on the yearly budget versus the actual expense on the line graph?
   B. What is the manufacturing strategy? Is it a one-shift, two-shift, or partial third-shift operation? How many hourly and salary personnel are involved?

C. The director of manufacturing is in charge of the in-process fabrication inventory. What are the total dollars and the inventory turns? What are the budgeted dollars versus the actual dollar amount? What are the budgeted inventory turns for fabrication versus the actual amount?

D. What are the lead times needed to be competitive in order to use speed as a competitive weapon in the marketplace? What is the lead time for customers in days?

E. What is the completion production rate versus the forecasted rate?

F. What is the actual (not adjusted) delivery percentage versus the customer's request?

G. What are the other key areas the director wishes to discuss?

7. Director of materials:

A. This position is separate and reports directly to the command center because of the major impact to material costs. The person must be aware of the opportunities and risk in working with overseas suppliers.

B. What are the purchased parts inventory dollars that are tied up? How do they relate to the budget? What are the inventory turns as related to the budget?

C. How many suppliers do you have? Using the 20/80 rule, which suppliers are in the 20% that equal 80% of the volume?

D. Are you using kanban controls to reduce lead times? What are your key lead times with suppliers?

E. What special programs do you have for the supplier's talents that involve design?

F. How much time is being lost due to lack of purchased parts? The objective should be 99% on-time delivery so that production schedules can be met.

G. Are there any other key areas or assistance for which the director of materials needs help?

8. Director of production engineering:

A. The director of production engineering combines the classic industrial engineering responsibilities with the traditional manufacturing engineering capabilities. This gives the director complete flexibility and accountability for all production processes.

B. What new processes are being investigated with product engineering?

C. What is the status of production tooling with regard to age of dies and fixtures? Is there a need to make updates with the help of industrial engineering?

D. The director of production engineering is also responsible for all kaizen events with the use of the industrial engineers and the strategic use of kanbans. What is the current status of these and the objectives?

E. Are there any other key areas or assistance for which the director of production engineering needs help?

9. Director of product engineering:

A. The director of product engineering is responsible for the innovation and design of products that marketing needs for the marketplace. He or she will work closely with input from marketing and sales.

B. This director must also work closely with production engineering to continually improve the capabilities and flexibilities of tooling.

C. The director of product engineering must be aware of all of the new material designs to reduce materials cost as much as possible. Working closely with production engineering, he or she must try to reduce the significant amount of parts needed to put into the product to reduce labor cost.

D. The director has to work closely with the materials area to assist suppliers in conforming to the standards they established.

E. This position is important because it involves input and work with practically every discipline on the command center. The leader must be innovative, passionate for success, a team player, and people oriented. It is not an easy position.

F. Are there any other key areas or assistance with which the director of product engineering needs help?

10. Director of sales:

A. A line chart showing the actual sales year to date versus the budget year to date should be used. On this same line chart, different colors should represent last year's sales and profits.

B. Include a chart showing the 20/80 rule on customers to identify from a team standpoint where the key customers are and discuss how to give them outstanding service.

C. Working closely with the competitive intelligence director, you should identify your top three competitors and list their weaknesses and strengths compared to your weaknesses and strengths. Discuss what can be done to exploit their weakness with your strengths while addressing defense. Address what needs to be done to strengthen your weaknesses.

D. Are there any other key areas of assistance with which the director of sales needs help?

11. Director of marketing:

A. Show a line chart depicting the share market from year to date versus the forecast.

B. A review of the organizational structure of sales versus key competition would again be accomplished with the help of the director of competitive intelligence.

C. Marketing gives the entire business the direction to accomplish the agreed-on objectives. the marketing department should be responsible for the pricing function.

D. Marketing should work closely with a director from competitive intelligence to understand what the real street price is and propose a strategy on pricing.

E. The marketing department, with inputs from the marketing director, sales director, and the competitive intelligence director, should work with the product engineering director in the design of new equipment to be competitive in the marketplace. This should include a target cost with a new product and input from the quality director. The new product needs to have the best quality in the marketplace. The product must not only perform outstandingly but also should be easy to service. It should set a standard for excellence and life expectancy.

F. Are there any problems or opportunities that should be discussed with the command center team?

12. Director of safety:

A. I have listed the director of safety as a separate director reporting to the command center because it is critical to send your people home in at least the same shape they came to work. You must have patience to watch over your people as a guardian of the workforce. Safety can be a key factor in the loss of needed personnel when they are injured. That could have a negative effect on production, particularly on quality to our customers, which is paramount.

B. Also important are injured employees, which can cause serious financial problems. Highlight their positioning and importance not to be subordinated to some other area, such as HR. HR is a critical function for the employees. I see them working closely together as a team.

C. When envisioning the command center, I see a line chart showing the lost hours that have occurred because of safety and a current record of accidents status. The same chart must include a comparison of last year's record to the current date.

D. The director of safety should give an overall report of areas of concern and where he or she needs assistance. This should be done to remove any hazards quickly. The other support teams in the overall command center should report on how they are going to make corrective actions in their areas.

E. If any employee's injury causes lost time, then the supervisor who is responsible for employees in the office, shop, or field must report the injury in the command center meeting regarding why the accident occurred and what is being done to correct it.

F. I believe the position of the director of safety reporting to the command center gives credence to the fact that team members and employees are a company's greatest asset. They always have priority over anything else being done.

G. Include any items to report to or questioned by the safety director that have not been covered.

13. Director of competitive intelligence (reports to the CFO and CEO):

A. The director of this new position reports to the command center because, as it is in combat, we cannot act without considering how the competition can retaliate or affect our operation. In today's worldwide competitive environment, it is even more important to find out how we can compete against enemies. I believe the position should consider the following: Working with marketing and sales as a team, agree on what your strengths and weaknesses are versus the top three competitors' top three strengths and weaknesses. You must give your inputs and considerations to the business command center as the objectives and tactics are reviewed.

B. Competitive intelligence should develop field input on competition from your salespeople in the field plus your customers in the field and the dealers and distributors you have in the field. They should issue a report on the top three competitors as they obtain feedback from their field of contacts. Radical change should be brought to the attention of the command center about a new competitor or something dramatic happening to other competitors beyond the top three.

C. This should be a highly confidential summary status issued monthly to a select group of directors, mainly sales, marketing, product engineering, and of course the commanders of the business command center.

D. Any strategies or marketing considerations that are new should be run by the competitive intelligence director to know what reaction might come from the field.

E. The director of competitive intelligence should monitor the pricing in the marketplace by competition and any intelligence on a lower price by a competitor because the competitor is in trouble regarding cash flow or overstocked inventories. This should be shared immediately with marketing, sales, and product engineering. If something dramatic should occur, then it should be brought to the attention of the command center.

F. The director of competitive intelligence should be able to bring any topic to the table he or she feels is critical to the recommendations of the business command center.

My suggestions for directors and who should attend the daily management control center meetings were reviewed. I included input regarding what I feel are core contributions by each director to the command center. You and your team will need to determine the best service for your team's style, culture, and business.

My thought is for the CEO and COO (chief operating officer) to review with their staff and change the makeup to the team's suggestion if needed. If it needs to be changed after a fair trial, make the change. But, the less changes that you make, the less confusion that you will have. So, make your studies of your organization as foolproof as possible.

How Do You Organize Control of the Command Center?

1. Finalize the topics you wish to review daily and the format of who goes first in the organization meeting. Use speed of information for quick reaction in addressing problems and opportunities.

2. Establish a daily agenda of priorities that need to be covered first because they are important. The screen managers will review key points with the CEO and CFO the day before a meeting for special instructions.

3. I believe there is a critical need to better manage the control center using three separate screens. There is so much detail that you should cover; having three screens and screen managers will add better control over what is being done.

4. Having control of the data in real time furthers the importance of having three screens and three screen managers.

The employee in charge of each screen is totally responsible for the topics assigned to his or her screen. The screen manager needs to have all of the updated information readily available at the 9 a.m. start of the meeting. This manager will individually coordinate his or her screen and handle the presentation in the control center. The directors must give priority to the corrections or the information needed for the following morning's 9 a.m. meeting in sufficient time so the screen manager will have it ready for presentation. This way, the director's valuable time is not wasted on training the presenter.

Each screen manager will have people on three shifts reporting to him or her separately. The screen manager will collect all information from the field and throughout the corporations. These managers' screens will be filled with important information for the following day.

It is important for all the directors to understand their obligation is to supply timely data to the screen managers. Each director is responsible to see that his or her people conform and have the necessary support for the following day. This must include the special action they suggest be taken, by whom, and when. Each screen manager will have an assistant reporting to him or her to take daily notes of the action that needs to be followed up and help expedite needed information. The screen manager's portion is critical because it becomes each director's responsibility.

5. I suggest a first-class telecommunications conference call system be included in the command center and a first-class recording machine that can pick up all of the conversations through speakers. The recording should be available in a library inside the command center for reference as needed.

6. The command center must have security so only a limited number of people are allowed in with their directors when needed. The security should also consist of a limited number of keys to access the command center. A security person will be available to allow a director into the command center for information updates 24 hours a day.

7. My next topic is the design of the command center itself. The space I suggest could result as a consequence of kaizen events or a reduction of inventory. The location of the command center will vary with each corporation and its desires.

8. The floor plan of the command center (Figure 2.2) should be a separate building beside the first floor of the factory. I recommend the building have a second floor to house the computers and the three screens. They are totally independent of each other and feed data to the command center. The second floor have the people on three shifts collecting the necessary data and receiving communications throughout the field as intelligence. The details from the field are a result of what the command center wishes to receive, but the more up-to-date communications are in real time, the bigger advantage you will have for using speed and flexibility as competitive weapons.

Special Note: As you break down the bureaucracy by the central use of the command center, you should have quite a few salary head counts that can be eliminated. The command center will eliminate at least 50% of the meetings taking place. Therefore, you should be able to have adequate head counts to man the command center's three shifts.

I want this book to be functional, not entertaining. Much information is covered. The purpose is to energize you and open your imagination to what could be. As I have said, you belong to a certain culture, and you will have to adapt what is in this book to your culture.

You are also at a certain point in evolution that is different from other people. You have different products that require different capabilities. You may already be doing many things well. So, you need to adapt these tools

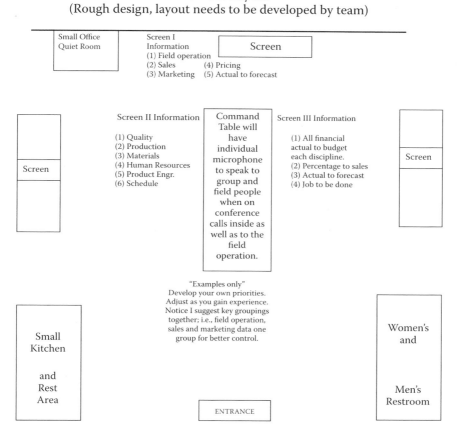

First Floor Layout
(Rough design, layout needs to be developed by team)

FIGURE 2.2
First floor layout.

to help you do even better. These are generalities that I wanted to include as a special note.

In my opinion, the most critical part of what I am suggesting is the selection and training of the screen managers. Please take this seriously. Your success or failure will depend on how you handle it. I purposefully narrowed it to three separate screens so that the screen manager would have time to make sure that all of the data that they are working with are correct. These individuals are the secret to the command center. If they are trained well and they execute their work properly with professional enthusiasm, they will be worth their weight in gold: Pay them well.

SECOND FLOOR
(layout needs to be developed by the team)

Second Floor Purpose

(1) Assign a leader for each screen. They are responsible to maintain computer and data input of their screen.

(2) They will have separate computer and storage for their screen.

(3) They must be responsible for all communication needed to update data 24 hours a day and seven days a week.

(4) They will need support people to accomplish this objective.

(5) Communication links will need to be established with the correct directors to maintain real-time data for their screen.

(6) Management must develop the "dashboard" approach where condition "Red" receives first priority at meetings. On major specific items, condition yellow will be reviewed to avoid reaching condition red.

(7) Screen leaders will be at a 9:00 A.M. meeting each day and present their screen update and answer all requests on specific data and capability to roll over to detail that supports presented data.

Small Kitchen and Rest Area	Women's and ——— Men's Restrooms

FIGURE 2.3
Second floor layout.

We must remember that the screen managers are taking the responsibility and accountability for their given areas. In doing so, they remove a tremendous amount of pressure and time preparation from the command staff. They must be accurate and timely. They need sufficient people reporting to them to ensure that everything is accurate and professional with no excuses.

I purposefully gave each an assistant. Once the screen manager has experience and is broken in, things will run much easier, and credibility will increase. Remember, the president and CEO are updated prior to each meeting, similar to the way the president of the United States is updated every morning.

The report to the executive must be summarized. There may be one or two things that are serious that must be resolved in the meeting. There may be some intelligence that need to be reported to them. Attached to this report would be items that are just nice to know (i.e., intelligence on the competition).

Again, the number of screen operators may depend on the size of your company. However, you do need at least two in case there is an absence. There is no question in my mind that communications needed will be quickly known to all members of the team. You need to decide how many operators you need and what you need them to do. Because of the critical nature of the command center, I suggest having it in a separate building with less interference and better security. You must adapt to your present situation.

I do feel strongly that we must do something with our industry to be competitive. Communication will be critical to its success. If it is done correctly, you will have more time to spend with customers or to work on critical strategies.

One other extremely important and valuable key point that you must recognize is that the factory and offices will be operating on a normal 5-day work week. But, the screen managers will operate 7 days a week. Saturdays and Sundays provide great opportunities for gaining intelligence from the field people, as expected. You can make your own list of what you expect. A suggested list would include the following:

How do your prices compare to the competition in the marketplace?
Is there a problem at one of the competitors that you should know about?
Has there been a change of management at the competition?
What problems are happening in the field that need to be addressed?

Having this time to receive information or calls from the field is a real advantage over the competition, who will not normally be communicating on Saturday and Sunday. Again, each organization has its own requirements. The more you know about the enemy, the better you can fight the war. I have said many times that speed is a competitive weapon. As you sharpen your abilities, you will obtain better intelligence to use.

Summary

I tried to have you think out of the box. I offered various suggestions and strategies as examples that you may consider:

A. Holding action has allowed you to have time to rethink the business.
B. There are approaches to consider in your rethinking of your business mission statement, objectives, strategies, and tactics that you need to develop.
C. I also introduced the revolutionary organization concept to eliminate time lost in bureaucracy.
D. In doing so, I also introduced the concept of circulatory management, which eliminates internal squabbling between various directors. These directors are normally in conflict over their objectives in a business situation.

I introduced you to the wingman approach. This imitates a World War II action by which fighter pilots flew in pairs to protect each other for the success of the mission.

I have paired the internal division of directors. As an incentive to work together to complete both objectives, I suggest 70% of an individual director's measurement be on completion of personal objectives, but 30% of his measurement is on the completion of his or her wingman's objectives. Therefore, team spirit can be built between two naturally competitive individuals. The chemistry from working together will bring mutual financial gain.

Certain positions of the directors were elevated to report to the command center instead of being subordinate in the old system. A new position I believe is critical was added: competitive intelligence. It is listed directly on the circulatory management chart. There will be full visibility and participation at the command center and will provide a resource for all directors to gather information on competitors. This will work not only work for sales and marketing strategies but also for cost and design of products, distribution, knowledge of the key leaders of the competition, and so forth. I believe the lack of the position in the past has cost proper actions.

I also organized a new concept referred to as a screen manager. This person is totally responsible to ensure information is available on the screen detail for the daily 9 a.m. meeting. Again, I emphasize that all directors are going to be held accountable for their screen information. It must be available for the meeting.

The critical concept of the command center stems from everyone being trained to do his or her job and support the screen manager, whose only responsibility is to coordinate and pass on the information that the directors or their people give them. The director stands responsible for his or her own area at all times.

E. A reality check at the end needs to be made. It may not be practical or possible to have the CEO and CFO present at every meeting because of their other responsibilities to the board and the customers. I suggest there might be a given day of the week when the structure is for them to be present to handle major decisions. In their absence, a subordinate will be fully authorized to take action on what is needed on that day that cannot wait.

In reality, there may be occasions when several directors cannot be available for good reasons. They also must have empowered subordinates at the meeting to make decisions. I mentioned that business is war, and war cannot just be put on hold until somebody shows up. The team at the command center must always take action in real time. After management has taken out the bugs in the system, there may be abbreviated portions of the meeting on serious problems. They could occur over a teleconference connected to the key decision makers so they can be alerted by the command center.

The good news is that by picking the right person to fill the position needed for decisions, it will test the individuals and build backup people for the manager when the manager is not present.

The command center is a real-time, living organization. It can be used throughout the day for presentations from management after the initial structured meeting is complete.

Last, all of these tools are meant for management to rethink what needs to be done and how it should be done. I have tried to do give you a skeleton for you to flesh out to management for your organization's specific needs. I want this to open your eyes to the future of what can be accomplished. I see this as only a foundation of what the future will be in laser light communications and responsibilities. There is too much information being generated from throughout the world. I believe it is beyond the control of one individual. At some point, you will have to revise the structure to focus on key items. A prevalent danger in today's business world occurs when management is expected to cover too many areas and therefore ceases to become an expert in all areas. That process leaves the danger of bad decisions and poor timing or no action, only reaction to the combat of daily business operations. I hope I have energized you to look at the different possibilities and adapt them as you see fit while maintaining the base of a command center after you have completed all of the homework suggested. I know I have asked you to consider a lot of changes.

You must outthink your competition, not just outwork them. If you only operate computers on ground rules, then you will surely lose.

Reading this book will not make you a success. It is what you do differently that will make you a success. Good luck and good hunting.

WHAT ARE THE BENEFITS OF HAVING A BUSINESS COMMAND CENTER?

The following are benefits of having a business command center:

1. Decisive and timely action will be taken in real time.
2. There will be a dramatic reduction of meetings.
3. Speed will be a competitive weapon.
4. All discussions in the command center can be recorded for follow-up and historical records.
5. All employees will be better prepared and more visually responsible to have needed information available when required.
6. The total team will be focused on the command center instructions and needs.
7. Productivity will be improved dramatically.
8. As in war, you will be continually under attack. Do not play defensively; but with all the timely information, you will be able to outplay and beat the opponent in the marketplace.
9. Communications are now shared with more of the total team. All key managers will now be on all communications and will have pride in being part of the team.
10. This system will reward the believers and remove the nonbelievers.

FUTURE POSSIBILITIES

The following discussion concerns what I call continuous improvement (kaizens). The dashboard approach is used to set priorities in this presentation. If you are not acquainted with the dashboard approach, make it a point to research more details about this approach, particularly if you have higher management responsibilities. Simplified, it sets up critical areas of the business (e.g., profitability or expenses, stock trends, etc.), whichever areas that you feel are critical priorities.

For example, financially, the CFO could set a weekly profitability rate to meet the financial forecast for the month. If you are ahead, it will show as green in the computer. But, more important, if you are behind in share market, red will show. The point is that the dashboard will let you set your own critical priorities. These would be the priorities to address at the command center. It is a fantastic tool if used properly for the critical areas as assessed by management. It also can be reduced into a different group, such as manufacturing. The plant manager could list the critical areas that he or she wants. If the dashboard indicator becomes red, everyone will notice. The bottom line is that it is a powerful tool for getting the attention of managers to alert them to do something. One feature that I like is that if an item is red for more than 24 hours, then it goes up the line to management. This encourages the team to react quickly.

To give the key executives flexibility to travel and still be accountable for the business command center, a portion of the command center's key decision makers can be brought together at a certain time and may have a teleconference with the executive in the field:

The command center meetings will always begin at exactly 9:00 a.m. They should be planned so they will conclude by 11:00 a.m.

If there is an emergency requiring more inputs in the field or someone else, then these cause exceptions to the end time of 11:00 a.m., and the meeting will extend to whatever time is necessary to resolve decision making regarding the exceptions. Those executives not needed will be excused.

The command center should also be used as needed for making presentations requested by the command center leaders after the conclusion of the command center's business for the day.

The three screen managers, as discussed previously, are responsible for the data presented on their screens. After the full presentation, they must maintain the follow-up and prepare the inputs for the following day's meeting to the various command center team members.

The choosing of the screen managers and their training are critical to the command center. They must be in charge of their screens and the data to be used. All members of the command center must give them full attention so that they are prepared for the next day for the items that are taking place in real time in the field.

The screen managers, using the dashboard approach, will work with the CFO to establish the objectives to be used for the dashboard to run the business, which simplifies the amount of items and accents the critical items.

The screen operator is responsible for key data for the screens and working in real time. If one of the measurements has a red indicator or completely misses the target, the operator must alert the team members to identify the problem quickly. If the command center leaders are not directly available, then they must be located. The leaders must give their final approval before an action is taken.

A spin-off of the command center may be a video conference with the full organization or other management teams at the same time.

Field Sales Organization

The field sales organization is a conduit between the customers and the management organization. It takes a certain type of individual to be a field salesperson. These individuals must have self-confidence and push themselves for success; they must be able to handle failure on occasion to reach an objective, then they must calm down and rethink a different approach to meet the objective in sales. This is a complex position. The work is not as easy as people think. These people have to deal with all sorts of personalities and fixed opinions. If that is not bad enough, they have to compete against competitors who are after the same victories. Each of us has personal strengths and weaknesses and must manage them in a society that is extremely complex with changing cultures.

The culture that we have today is influenced by who you know to get in the door to meet the right people. A better product does not always get you the sale. The business world is becoming smaller and more complex.

I think in the future we must help salespeople be successful. One of the ways is to have individuals in HR go out in the field and meet with salespeople in their territory and find out what help they could provide for their success. We do not want more meetings. We need to add certain people to the HR team for success. The HR team should be neutral, not push marketing, sales, or finance. While maintaining confidentiality, the team should help each individual in the field become more confident and successful. On the other hand, business-wise, we should invite various salespeople in the field to call the command center at a specific time to discuss what can be done to help fight the competition. By calling the command center, all of the people will be there for the various areas in which the salesperson needs help. This allows instant communications without barriers. It gives the field salesperson access that is not normally available. From this communication, an action plan can be developed to help this person. It is a powerful tool to help boost business. The most powerful weapons in business are our people and their abilities. We must remove all obstacles for the salesperson to assist the company in winning the order.

I think in business today we must shift our gears to a lower speed depending on the occasion. We must be calm, cool, and calculating as a team. This is uncharted territory regarding what it should be and how it is controlled.

Distribution Centers

We need to rethink what a distribution center is. Basically, other than technology improvements, the mission is the same as obtaining product from manufacturing and selling it to customers. I have said this before, but it is important to say again. You should make all communications through the computer with standard forms for sales entry, warranty, and so on. This should eliminate all paperwork. This will create a history, sometimes more than you want. I would like to see distributors get together as a team regionally so that it may be more effective.

The purpose of gathering the distributors is to find out what you can do to make their lives easier, what you can do to steal orders from the competition, and how financially can you help them reduce cost. For example, how effective is floor planning or consigning inventory?

We are in the middle of a quiet revolution that management may not recognize. You must make distribution effective and consumer oriented.

Distributors are like Broadway actors. They are on stage with their customers. They are on stage with their customers. They need to be trained on how to make their customers like them more.

I once had management list the SKUs in descending order volume-wise and then list the profitability in descending order. There is a tremendous amount of money to be made in distribution and manufacturing. If this is done, management will see that there are some SKUs that have small volumes. It is beneficial if you can take these units and tell the customer that you can provide a similar model at a discount to do away with the troublesome small-run SKUs. If the customer does not want to do it, you increase the price dramatically; normally, that changes the customer's mind. If management would do this, they would see a tremendous amount of savings. Normally, the fewer SKUs there are, the better off you are financially.

CLOSING THOUGHTS

Remember it is not what you read that is important. It is what you *do* that counts. I want each of you to win this war. I want to leave you with the Marine Corps' orders to apply as needed:

Improvise
Adapt
Overcome

If you have any questions, call me directly on my private line at (865) 681-0029 or e-mail me at roger@wcconsultants.com, and I will be glad to answer them at no cost. If you wish for us to join your team to help implement any item, we would be glad to do so.

Roger G. Lewandowski, CEO
World Competition Consultants

FURTHER INFORMATION AND HOMEWORK

FIGURE 2.4
Toyota Seven Wastes and Japanese Six Ss.

Specialists in rapid implementation

FIGURE 2.5
Eight office wastes.

Use of obsolete job description
Use of obsolete processes
Duplications
Average productivity of 55% in an office force
Too many chiefs
Lack of trained supervisors
Lack of motivation
Very slow and not flexible

Our mission is not to eliminate people; our mission is to eliminate waste at every level and help those in management reinvent their organizations using speed as a competitive weapon.

As outside people, we have no vested interest or political involvement, which are obstacles in many organizations.

TOYOTA SEVEN WASTES OF MANUFACTURING

Transportation

Overproduction

Motion

Process itself

Inventory

Waiting

Making Defective Products

Contact: _____

Company: _____

Address: _____

City/State: _____ Zip: _____

Assessment date: _____

Specialists in rapid implementation

FIGURE 2.6
Assessment form.

Toyota's 7 Manufacturing Wastes:
Transportation/Conveyance

Specialists in rapid implementation

Supervisor Name:
Area:

Observation:

Good Things:

Needs Improvement:

New Ideas:

Supervisor Name:
Area:

Observation:

Good Things:

Needs Improvement:

New Ideas:

Supervisor Name:
Area:

Observation:

Good Things:

Needs Improvement:

New Ideas:

Supervisor Name:
Area:

Observation:

Good Things:

Needs Improvement:

New Ideas:

FIGURE 2.7
Assessment form (continued).

Toyota's 7 Manufacturing Wastes:
Overproduction

Specialists in rapid implementation

Supervisor Name: Area: Observation: Good Things: Needs Improvement: New Ideas:	Supervisor Name: Area: Observation: Good Things: Needs Improvement: New Ideas:
Supervisor Name: Area: Observation: Good Things: Needs Improvement: New Ideas:	Supervisor Name: Area: Observation: Good Things: Needs Improvement: New Ideas:

FIGURE 2.8
Assessment form (continued).

Toyota's 7 Manufacturing Wastes:
Excess Motion (of operator/machine)

Specialists in rapid implementation

3

SupervisorName: **Area:** Observation: Good Things: Needs Improvement: New Ideas:	SupervisorName: **Area:** Observation: Good Things: Needs Improvement: New Ideas:
SupervisorName: **Area:** Observation: Good Things: Needs Improvement: New Ideas:	SupervisorName: **Area:** Observation: Good Things: Needs Improvement: New Ideas:

FIGURE 2.9
Assessment form (continued).

Toyota's 7 Manufacturing Wastes:
Defects (rework/scrap)

Specialists in rapid implementation

Supervisor Name: Area: Observation: Good Things: Needs Improvement: New Ideas:	Supervisor Name: Area: Observation: Good Things: Needs Improvement: New Ideas:
Supervisor Name: Area: Observation: Good Things: Needs Improvement: New Ideas:	Supervisor Name: Area: Observation: Good Things: Needs Improvement: New Ideas:

FIGURE 2.10
Assessment form (continued).

**Toyota's 7 Manufacturing Wastes:
Inventory (raw material)**

Specialists in rapid implementation

Supervisor Name: **Area:**
Observation:
Good Things:
Needs Improvement:
New Ideas:

Supervisor Name: **Area:**
Observation:
Good Things:
Needs Improvement:
New Ideas:

Supervisor Name: **Area:**
Observation:
Good Things:
Needs Improvement:
New Ideas:

Supervisor Name: **Area:**
Observation:
Good Things:
Needs Improvement:
New Ideas:

FIGURE 2.11
Assessment form (continued).

Toyota's 7 Manufacturing Wastes:
Waiting (of operator or machine)

Specialists in rapid implementation

Supervisor Name:
Area:

Observation:

Good Things:

Needs Improvement:

New Ideas:

Supervisor Name:
Area:

Observation:

Good Things:

Needs Improvement:

New Ideas:

Supervisor Name:
Area:

Observation:

Good Things:

Needs Improvement:

New Ideas:

Supervisor Name:
Area:

Observation:

Good Things:

Needs Improvement:

New Ideas:

FIGURE 2.12
Assessment form (continued).

Toyota's 7 Manufacturing Wastes:
Process Itself/Overprocessing

Specialists in rapid implementation

SupervisorName:
Area:
Observation:
Good Things:
Needs Improvement:
New Ideas:

SupervisorName:
Area:
Observation:
Good Things:
Needs Improvement:
New Ideas:

SupervisorName:
Area:
Observation:
Good Things:
Needs Improvement:
New Ideas:

SupervisorName:
Area:
Observation:
Good Things:
Needs Improvement:
New Ideas:

FIGURE 2.13
Assessment form (continued).

BONUS: SAFETY

Specialists in rapid implementation

Supervisor Name: **Area:** Observation: Good Things: Needs Improvement: New Ideas:	**Supervisor Name:** **Area:** Observation: Good Things: Needs Improvement: New Ideas:
Supervisor Name: **Area:** Observation: Good Things: Needs Improvement: New Ideas:	**Supervisor Name:** **Area:** Observation: Good Things: Needs Improvement: New Ideas:

FIGURE 2.14
Assessment form (continued).

Key process identification and process review

Specialists in rapid implementation

Name of facility:_____

Date:_____

Description of process:_____
_____
_____

1. Is capacity constrained?_____
   Can it be improved? If so, how?
   _____
   _____
   _____

2. Is quality excellent?_____
   If not, how can it be improved?
   _____
   _____
   _____

3. Does plant layout have the right things in the right places?_____
   If not, what do we recommend be done?
   _____
   _____
   _____

   WCC Representative:_____

FIGURE 2.15
Key process identification form.

ADVANCED VALUE STREAM MAPPING

Facility: _____

Study Process: _____

By: _____ Date: _____

I. Summarize Present Job Description (If a job description is available, request to save for reference):

_____

_____

II. Purpose:

_____

_____

III. Time to Perform:

_____

_____

IV. Production Estimate of Job Work Content (6-hour job, 8-hour job, etc.): Evaluate (Use 5-question approach; "evaluation of step in process")

A. Is it still needed?

_____

B. Can it be combined with another step? (May have to answer later in process)

_____

C. Can you eliminate wasted time?

_____

D. How long does it take now?

_____

E. How can you reduce the time? (New methods, ideas, formats)

_____

Inputs of Step 1 in process for Step 2:

General comments:

_____

_____

_____

_____

Specialists in rapid implementation

RAPID IMPROVEMENT CHECKLIST

The following is a checklist to aid in preparing for a Rapid Improvement Event.

Target Area Selection:
- What are the relevant business needs or objectives? _____
- What are the candidate RI areas? _____
- Which (ones) of these are selected? _____
- How does selection of these areas support business needs or objectives? _____
- Have any of these areas been previously improved? _____

Gathering Performance Data:
- What is recent performance of the area to be improved?

	Measure	Trend (positive/negative/flat)
• Quality	_____	_____
• Delivery	_____	_____
• Productivity	_____	_____
• Cost	_____	_____
• Overtime	_____	_____
• Other _____	_____	_____
• Other _____	_____	_____

- What performance measures are below minimum standards?

Setting the Objectives:
- What are the most pressing business needs related to this area?_____
- Improvements:

Target Area	How will improvement in target area be measured?
_____	_____
_____	_____
_____	_____
_____	_____
_____	_____
_____	_____

- What are the (tentative) objectives?

Target Area	Current Performance	Objective
_____	_____	_____
_____	_____	_____
_____	_____	_____
_____	_____	_____
_____	_____	_____
_____	_____	_____

- Has management signed off on improvement areas, measure and objectives? _____
- What is the single most important metric to use as an indicator of "holding the gains?"_____
  _____

FIGURE 2.16
Rapid improvement checklist.

<u>**Team Selection:**</u>

- What skills or knowledge are required?
  - Leadership   _____
  - Equipment operation _____
  - Assembly   _____
  - Creativity   _____
  - Analytical   _____
  - Time and motion   _____
  - Material handling   _____
  - Fresh look   _____
  - Programming   _____
  - Other_____   _____

- What departments, jobs or shifts need representation?
  - Area Supervision   _____
  - Operators   _____
  - 1st, 2nd & 3rd shifts   _____
  - Supplier   _____
  - Customer   _____
  - Engineering   _____
  - Purchasing   _____
  - Scheduling   _____
  - Data processing   _____
  - Materials   _____
  - Quality   _____
  - Other_____   _____
- Have team members been selected?_____ Primary team? _____ Support team? _____
- Have selections been approved/sanctioned? _____
- Have participants, support personnel and affected people been informed?_____

<u>**Team Leader's Orientation and Preparation**</u>

- Teamleader orientation   _____
- Teamleader's notebook   _____
- Collect operation data   _____
- Calculate TAKT time   _____
- Prepare event objectives and results sheet   _____
- Prepare team leaders initial game plan   _____
- Communicate with those in area to be improved   _____

<u>**Preparation for Training**</u>

- Training location reserved?   _____
- Room setup   _____
- Audio/Visual equipment   _____
- Special exercise preparation   _____
- Notebooks   _____

<u>**Other Preparations**</u>

- Administrative items: Work hours? Overtime? Pay? Meals? Dress code? _____
- Video equipment   _____
- Cameras, extra batteries   _____
- Stop watches   _____
- Special materials   _____
- Maintenance services   _____

FIGURE 2.17
Rapid improvement checklist (continued).

GUIDELINE RECOMMENDATIONS:
WORKPLACE ORGANIZATION / 5 Ss

Ratings: **0** = Doesn't meet standard/expectation   **1** = Meets standard/expectation

ITEM	DESCRIPTION	0	1
1	Remove unnecessary items that will not be used in a timely manner.		
2	All cleaning equipment stored in a neat manner.		
3	All floors are clean of debris and free of oil and excess dirt.		
4	All safety equipment is in good working order and available for immediate use.		
5	Aisles are clear and not being used for storage.		
6	Storage boxes, containers and work in process are neat and in their marked locations.		
7	Machines are clean of excess oil, guards are in place and no visible defects.		
8	All necessary tools are present, conveniently located and neatly arranged.		
9	Bulletin boards are neatly arranged, and visible tracking charts are up to date.		
10	Work orders are staged and properly arranged for upcoming work.		
11	Personnel items are not present in the work area.		
12	Leaks have been identified with leak tags.		
13	Cabinets are neat and clean with NO loose items stored on top.		
14	Tool boxes are clean.		
15	Material identified at QS-9000 level.		
16	Chip barrel location and type of scrap are clearly identified.		
17	Trash containers are clean and stored in their designated location.		
18	Area has adequate lighting for operator to perform their job.		
19	Cardboard and wood are stored in designed areas with no overflow.		
20	Would you want to bring a CCP customer to this area?		

Question:

| 21 | **With sequence build establish how many ahead can material be delivered?** **May want to check to see if that is being adhered to on this audit form.** | | |

TOTAL SCORE:

18–20 pts	**Excellent**
15–17 pts	**Average**
12–14 pts	**Below average**
9–11 pts	**Needs work immediately**
8 or less	**Shut down and clean area up!**

FIGURE 2.18
Guideline for workplace organization.

Lean Manufacturing: Savings in Dollars

	Jan	Feb	March	April	May	June	July	Aug	Sep	Oct	Nov	Dec
Office												
Sales												
Marketing												
Product engineering												
Manufacturing engineering												
Industrial engineering												
Assembly												
Pressroom												

The Lean manufacturing coach and coordinator is responsible for submitting this monthly savings report on each department to the general manager. Also, each employee is encouraged to place money-saving ideas in a suggestion box. Every idea used is entered into drawings for prizes.

Checking Trend: Total Department Expenses

	Office	Sales	Marketing	Manufacturing	Warehouse	Engineering	Quality
2011							
2012							
2013							
2014 to date							

Checking Trend: Total Sales per Employee and Total Sales versus Wages (in dollars)

	Total Sales ($)	Total Number of Employees	Ratio	Total Sales per Employee	Total Sales/ Total Wages
2011					
2012					
2013					
2014 to date					

Space Ratio versus Sales

	Space (ft²)	Sales Volume	Employee Cost ($)	Sales Volume per Square Foot	Employee Cost per Square Foot
2011					
2012					
2013					
2014 to date					

ACCOUNTING: THE DICTATORS OF CORPORATIONS OR FORGOTTEN PRIESTS? WHAT SHOULD ITS ROLE BE?

The accounting function is as critical to the success of a company as a compass is to a ship at sea. It must be remembered, though, that a compass tells you your direction, but not how to get where you are going.

The proper balance is essential, and in the business world of today, if accounting or the accounting approach is a major power in an organization, then the success of an organization in global combat might be short-lived. The marketplace is not so simple that it can be run by calculations, ratios, or trends. The marketplace is emotional, is not always logical, and certainly is highly unpredictable. If too much emphasis is put on the accounting approach, the organization can turn into an even bigger bureaucracy than it currently is, with studies on studies for the justification of any action considered. Running a corporation trickily by the numbers will not give the flexibility and expediency needed in the marketplace.

On the other hand, there are some organizations that, outside core requirements for financial reporting for government requirements, tend to ignore account involvement. They partition them off in their own area and restrict them to it. Consideration is only given to them when there is a desire to influence or juggle numbers being reported. There are cute phrases like "bean counters" or "green shade people" used to describe people in accounting in this type of negative organization.

I have mentioned that one of the ways to control overhead cost and to maintain the state of the art in accounting is to outsource as much as possible those accounting functions that lend themselves to this approach. If this is not desirable or practical in an organization, then a fresh look at the accounting mission should be made. In accounting, someone should deal with the real numbers and have the integrity to keep them honest so that the pulse of the organization can be taken from a financial standpoint. Those in accounting must perform this task with the integrity of a priest or minister, and they should be held in the same esteem in that they should deal with the truth. When report figures are negative, we should not try to influence them to change them or use a "kill-the-messenger" approach when responding to such reports. They should have the respect of all of management, and they should work closely with management to give advice and counsel to each manager in his or her own area. They should also maintain the integrity and confidentiality of conversations between themselves and the various line managers regarding possible problems and solutions and not spread gossip or report problem areas to everyone in the cafeteria.

One of the ways of measuring the real power and potential of accounting is to take down the walls behind which they operate. In most places today, accounting departments are centralized and should be decentralized to the extent that the only things left centralized are the core functions required to issue the various financial reports to top management and to government agencies.

This does not mean that a decentralized accounting department would continue the normal functions with just a new boss. These accounting people, whether they are now part of engineering, personnel, marketing, or manufacturing, should be brought into discussions and contribute their expertise at the onset. For example, on costing of new designs, they should be involved in evaluating the cost of marketing programs for marketing people; they should be involved in assisting personnel to monitor fringe costs and wage programs and to assist in contract negotiations. In manufacturing, they should counsel in areas that, based on figures, need attention and should be part of the forces to address these problems. They would also review all capital tooling costs with manufacturing to decide if the money should be spent for tooling and its effect on profitability if it is purchased to justify the decisions that are made.

These are a few examples of the point that when you do away with the traditional accounting department and procedures and place these people in an area where they are actively contributing to success, not just reappointing success or failure, your overall organization becomes much more effective. This approach should not only broaden the experience of the accounting people but also would remove the traditional view of those in accounting as "watchdogs" and help them acquire a new status as participants in the details of running the business. This would broaden their knowledge and contribute to better decision making; it would also train these very important people for future management positions while assisting the people they work with to proper financial analysis of situations. I think that this would be a win-win strategy because the quality of life for the accounting people would not be as structured; they would be active participants in the exciting world of the business itself.

U.S. PRODUCT ENGINEERING: IS IT A MISDIRECTED MISSILE AS IT IS NOW ORGANIZED?

The product engineering departments of the United States have been the envy of the world, having led the world with a steady stream of new products and outstanding accomplishments. Perhaps the zenith of this new engineering effort was when the United States was able to send a man to the moon and bring him back. Today, there is at least a question mark regarding whether U.S. engineering is still the leader. The Japanese have outengineered the mighty car industry to a point that American manufacturers are forced to look at joint ventures or components or give up the engineering effort and have the Japanese build the entire car for them. This is true in numerous other products that once were the private domain of U.S. concerns. It is not only the Japanese who should cause concern, but also the Germans, the Italians, and currently the Koreans. The third-world nations have sent scores of students to the best universities, not only in the United States but also throughout the world, to develop their engineering efforts and then to return home and help generate new industries for global competition.

These uncomfortable realizations about deteriorating U.S. leadership should cause us to rethink our engineering efforts. Some may say the problem is that the other countries spend much more money on engineering functions, both in equipment and in the larger number of engineers they have. But, in the final analysis, it is not the quantity of engineers that makes one successful, but the quality of the engineering effort. If we look at Edison, Ford, and Einstein, these men constantly accomplished enormous feats with relatively little help. In today's age, we can look at the Apple computer and many other modern-day success stories that were started in garages or small departments by brilliant engineers. There is one thread that is consistent between these people of the past and the people of today who are making breakthroughs in every engineering aspect of our lives, and it is that they were and are totally committed to their efforts. They were not swayed or influenced by any other objective, but concentrated their time and energy totally on what they planned to attain.

The question I am posing is as follows: Is U.S. engineering really organized for results in today's world, or is it a misdirected missile that is off course and in a self-destruct mode?

In our country, we have massive engineering departments and elaborate buildings and offices with the best equipment money can buy. So, what is the problem? I think we are perhaps overindulging and influencing the engineering people and, like good parents who are disappointed in their children, ask ourselves, Where did we go wrong?

One thing that we have done unconsciously in the effort to bring better communications between marketing, manufacturing, and engineering is to bring them into a jungle of bureaucracy and politics. We have distracted them and their creative people, who do not understand or want to be involved in bureaucracies and politics. The result of this distraction has lowered the efficiency of engineering, has stifled the creativeness of its people, and too often has influenced them to be a 9-to-5 society.

We must step back now while we still have some time and see where we should be going and correct our course before it is too late. I have some suggestions that may not be popular, but I think they are worthy of thought before they are discarded:

1. If at all possible, locate product engineering away from company or corporate headquarters. Get them away from the bureaucracy and politics and their related environment. Locate them, if possible, in a rural area so it is easier for them to get to work and to come back to work after hours and on weekends. The facility should be an attractive facility, campus-like or on a lake, but extremely informal. The atmosphere should be results oriented and in an environment that allows both of these things to exist. Politics would be unimportant, but achievements would be very important, and much should be made of them. Superawards should be given to those individuals or teams who have earned them. It might be said that this would isolate them from the marketing and manufacturing functions—that is the objective. It would not mean that there would not be liaisons with marketing and manufacturing; with today's instant communication, a network could be established to fill the need. Again, this should be as informal as it can be, with one-on-one relationships, fewer large meetings, and a minimum of paperwork.

2. There should be the opportunity for the engineers to have some quiet time to really think about their projects. They should be left alone with less-structured days so that they can concentrate on the

products or objectives they are trying to attain and communicate with their peers for consideration on how they might attain them.

3. Anyone being promoted in engineering from the original job entry should be promoted only because he or she produces tangible results that could both be seen and measured. If a new individual comes on board and outproduces a more senior person, that person is the one who should be promoted. Seniority or politics should not be a factor. This culture that rewards only achievements must be nurtured, not only in promotions, but also in pay. Everyone should be paid a very acceptable competitive wage. Those who produce more should be paid more; again, seniority is not a consideration. This recognition of the engineering people would make achievement the cornerstone of the engineering effort; as a result, this would make people more self-motivated and results oriented, regardless of the time they had worked for the company.

4. In the real world, there are brilliant engineers who would and do make poor managers. Could you imagine what kind of manager Einstein would have made in today's world? We must not destroy or misuse people with unusual creative abilities by making them managers so that they can be paid properly. We should have a special system based on tangible results that has various plateaus so that each and every person can reach a pay level that might well exceed that of the product engineering manager if their results are that good.

These special people might only have one or two assistants or perhaps they are by themselves. They are given special earned privileges and, to a great degree, a latitude regarding what they are working on. These people should have personal contact and reassurance at the highest level of the company or corporation to ensure that they would not be burdened by any bureaucracy.

5. Every engineering department should have its own "experimental section" that would vary in size based on the company or corporation size. This group uses the team approach to work on projects that are not part of a product plan for today.

There should not be any pressure for an early completion date, but these individuals should be given projects, in a broad sense, that either they propose or that are assigned by a steering committee whose membership depends on the company or corporate management structure. The objective is to work on something that represents *tomorrow's* market. Once given general guidelines, they would have total freedom regarding how they address this challenge, using all the latest technology available. They would report on a monthly basis to the steering committee concerning the progress of their projects and to obtain advice or counsel based on the status of the projects.

6. In the global world of competition, there are many excellent engineers located throughout the world, and they might not choose to relocate to the United States to look for employment. Today, with the ability to travel to any part of the world quickly and instant communications through electronics, it is not necessarily a prerequisite to have all your engineering talent located in the same building or area. A suggestion might be that you find out who the best engineering people in the world are for every facet of your engineering department. Even consider setting up small engineering cells in various parts of the world where these talented people could work on areas of their own expertise and then tie in their efforts to the network of the projects. It might not only be more suitable for these brilliant engineering people to work in their own country or environment but also might end up being less costly than to centralize them in one facility. We not only must think of engineering globally but also must break it down into areas of various expertise for each engineering function.

7. If you cannot hire the people who are the best globally, contract them for special projects or for consultation on problem solving. An additional benefit of these people is not only their expertise and a fresh look at opportunities, but also the fact that they are segmented might be a positive factor because their thinking is not influenced by talk of what cannot be done.

8. A forgotten asset in the United States, but not in Japan, is the proper use of suppliers, who, in Japan, play an important part in not only the manufacturing of products but also their development. An engineering relationship should be established with at least your key suppliers so that there is a dialogue regarding the state-of-the-art technology and its application to the product you are designing.

This additional engineering talent gives you a special resource and expertise to utilize at no additional cost. As a relationship develops between the two engineering departments, there would be a free flow of assistance that would, in the final analysis, make your product more competitive with world-class manufacturing costs and world-class quality.

This review of engineering recognizes that the mission of engineering is to serve the ultimate customers through the direction of the marketing department; in order to obtain the requested results, it must have excellent communications with manufacturing as well as marketing. In recognizing these basic principles, what I suggest here is that engineering should be allowed to go back and do the things those in engineering do best: be professional engineers. Their competition is allowed to do this and, in fact, encouraged to do this globally. If we are not careful in the United States, we will not only be outnumbered globally in engineering but also, regardless of the number, be outengineered.

INDUSTRIAL ENGINEERING: THE FORGOTTEN FUNCTION?

In 1903, Frederick Taylor wrote a paper, "Shop Management*." This was a significant breakthrough in terms of manufacturing. His concept was to determine the best way to do factory-related work, and he measured his results through the use of a stopwatch in time studies of the operations. This was an important breakthrough because the labor component of manufactured products was significant. In the years since then, the stopwatch has become pretty much obsolete with the introduction of methods outlined in manufacturing into rates per hour, per day, and so on. These systems provide a quick and consistent means of calculating shop floor rates and establishing standards. Today, with the use of automation and robotics, the labor component of products is being reduced significantly, and with increasing frequency, the work performed is becoming process controlled, with the operator only feeding or unloading the process. The actual labor component is reduced in many cases to less than 10% of product cost. I have called industrial engineering the forgotten function because, in many cases, management has forgotten its purpose. Many people and their associated costs are tied up to chase a small portion of the total product cost. These functions have been the present mode for a long time, with failure to reevaluate their purpose. In general, industrial engi-

---

* *Shop Management, The Principles of Scientific Management and Testimony before the Special House Committee,* by Frederick Winslow Taylor, Harper & Row, 1911.

neers have not on their own reassessed their mission and how they could better contribute to an organization.

Actually, there are some exciting areas in which industrial engineers could become involved and raise their profession to new heights. Let me offer an alternative to today's typical functions. First, there will always be a need for a benchmark to measure labor efficiency or an automated process in determining cost and a standard for people to attain. But, in today's environment, where there are numerous computer-assisted means of accomplishing this, we are wasting talent to have a graduate engineer perform this function or track it. This could be accomplished by using a 2-year graduate, who would enjoy the challenge and cost less.

The industrial engineering function should address the following areas:

1. Work with manufacturing engineering to establish the best method and flow for the manufacturing of components for a product being built or planned.
2. Now that the materials content of products has become a major cost factor for these products, reaching 75% or better, product components purchased should be evaluated and the buyer supported with estimates of the cost and producing them. They should visit key suppliers to gain firsthand knowledge of the processes and be a part of a purchasing team on all negotiations.
3. Identify areas where point-of-use manufacturing could be used and work with manufacturing engineering in its implementation.
4. Make surveys of handling being done within manufacturing. An example would be to make a list of components, both purchased and manufactured, and then determine how many times a part is being handled before it reaches the final assembly process. The object would be to reduce the number of times the part is handled, thereby reducing the cost of these occurrences that have no value added. In the process of making this analysis, the elimination of handling would also affect the amount of material handling of equipment required in a plant. Reinstatement of flowcharts would highlight these occurrences, and they would serve as a tool for corrective action.
5. Using their industrial engineering skills, these individuals would work with the salaried department heads and data-processing personnel first to eliminate and then automate as much of the paperwork functions as possible. Industrial engineering has spent too little time evaluating the salaried workforce and their methods. Next to

the materials cost, in most cases, these costs exceed direct labor costs. Too often, this area is ignored except when outside consultants are hired. Industrial engineers could and should take an active part in this area.

The key point is that the industrial engineering department could play a major role that would be more challenging than its present form and could contribute significantly to the overall pretax. This reassessment is necessary regardless of the size of your organization; once the industrial engineering people are given a clean sheet of paper to help determine their future, they could well add to the list of suggestions already made.

Index

A

accelerated return on kaizen (ARK), 24–27

accounting function, *see also* Financial leadership
    overview, 82–83
    zero-based process mapping, 19

action plans, 7–8, *see also specific tool*

A items and models, 11, 29–30

A Revolution in Manufacturing: The SMED System, 14

ARK, *see* Accelerated return on kaizen (ARK)

armed forces examples, 40, 44

assessment forms, 67–75

author contact information, 3, 64

automation, 1, 88

awards, 10–11, 85

B

backup areas, 16, 31

"bakery theory," 23

bandages for problems, 21, 24, *see also* Kanbans

basic resources, future trends, 38–39

"bean counters," *see* Accounting function

before and after summarization, 19

benchmarking, 89

benefits
    business command center, 60
    consolidation, 17
    kanbans, 24
    pull systems, 11
    working capital reduction, 6

B items and models, 30

bottlenecks, 13

bottling industries, 14

brainstorming, action plans, 9

bread-and-butter items, 7

Broadway actors example, 64

"buddy system" influence, *see* "Who you know" influence

building *vs.* planning schedule, 21

build it, they will come mindset, 11

bureaucracy impact, 41–42, 54, 85

"burn the ships" example, 45

business command center
    benefits, 60
    chart key points, 42–44
    circulatory management, 42–45
    conference call system, 54
    control organization, 52–57
    distribution centers, 63–64
    field sales organization, 62–63
    future trends, 61–64
    implementation, 41–42
    leadership, 45–52
    meetings, 61
    overview, 35–41
    secret to, 55
    security, 54
    space design, 54
    summary, 58–60

business plan, rethinking, 1, 3

buy *vs.* make, 24, *see also* Purchased parts

C

changeovers, *see* Single-minute exchange of dies (SMED)

changes, 1, 3, 36

China, future trends, 38–39

circulatory management
    chart, 43
    key points, 42–44
    overview, 42, 58

C items and models, 30–31

command center, *see* Business command center

commitment, 84

communication importance, 57

competitive information specialists
    core contributions, 51–52